HELL
A FINAL
WORD

HELL
A FINAL
WORD

The Surprising Truths I Found in the Bible

EDWARD WILLIAM FUDGE

LEAFWOOD
PUBLISHERS

an imprint of Abilene Christian University Press

HELL: A FINAL WORD
The surprising truths I found in the Bible

LEAFWOOD
P U B L I S H E R S
an imprint of Abilene Christian University Press

Copyright 2012 by Edward William Fudge

ISBN 978-089112-149-7
LCCN 2012010817

Printed in the United States of America

Quotations from the Bible are translated by the author.

LIBRARY OF CONGRESS CATALOGING-IN-PUBLICATION DATA
Fudge, Edward.
 Hell : a final word : the surprising truths I found in the Bible / Edward William Fudge.
    p. cm.
 ISBN 978-0-89112-149-7
 1. Hell--Biblical teaching. I. Title.
 BS680.H43F925 2012
 236'.25--dc23

                                                                      2012010817

Cover design by Marc Whitaker
Interior text design by Sandy Armstrong

Leafwood Publishers
ACU Box 29138
Abilene, Texas 79699
1-877-816-4455 toll free

For current information about all Leafwood titles, visit our Web site:
www.leafwoodpublishers.com

TO MOTHER

Known to the world as Sybil Short Fudge Dewhirst:

The personification of
   godly devotion,
   humble service,
   Christlike selflessness,
   and faithful loyalty;

She preached by pattern,
   taught by example,
   and loved without boundaries or discrimination.

She risked her life to give me mine—
   Invested her reputation in my defense;
Whom I can never repay,
   but who never expected that anyway.

Edward

ACKNOWLEDGEMENTS

This book calls for special words of appreciation to:

Jackie Lyles, who suggested it,
Leonard Allen, who requested it,
Jesse Ward, who brainstormed it,
Mark Lanier, who sponsored it, and
Sara Faye Fudge, who edited it.

*Thank you, and God bless you,
one and all,*

Edward William Fudge

"Hell was not made for men.
It is in no sense parallel to heaven;
It is 'the darkness outside,'
the outer rim where being fades away
into nonentity."

C. S. Lewis, *The Problem of Pain*

CONTENTS

MY INVITATION TO YOU

No doubt about it . . . HELL is a hot topic. And whatever they say on the subject, it seems almost everyone has an opinion. On one side of the aisle, promising sunny days and fair skies now and forever, are the television gurus, New Age evangelists and outright skeptics. On the other side we find prophets and priests, preachers and pundits—in full agreement as to hell's reality, while still debating the precise details.

If, like me, you take the Bible seriously (whether or not you also take it literally), you know that hell is part of its vision of the final future. That means we also must take hell into account in our own understanding of Last Things, else we will find ourselves looking at a distorted picture when measured by the book we all claim to follow.

That, of course, will require much thought—which itself calls for certain preparation if we are to do it well. Chief among those preparations, I suggest, are an open Bible, an open heart, and an open mind. Come join me with all three and let's see what surprises might await!

1 HELL FIRE AND HELL FEAR

I was only a fourth-grader, for heaven's sake, but the whirlpool of hellish fears that threatened to drown me seemed no less real based on my tender years on earth. And the panic—it was the kind you feel in a nightmare, the kind in which you are being chased by slimy, stinking, flesh-eating monsters, already breathing down your neck and gaining ground in hot pursuit. Perhaps you think it strange for a ten-year-old to be pondering hell in the first place. Especially—and can you believe it—on the day of his *baptism?*

The thought of facing God in judgment unbaptized scared the bejeebers out of me. Not because I thought that the physical event itself could forgive sins. Nor did I imagine that the gospel ordinance puts God in our debt or obligates him to do anything good in response (Rom. 11:33-36).

No, it was all about uniting with Jesus in the likeness of his burial and resurrection (Rom. 6:3-4). Baptism was the way faith jumped into the arms of God, trusting that Jesus' blood would wash away sins (Col. 2:12; Acts 22:16). This was not "baptismal regeneration," not magic, not "sacramentalism," as that word is properly used. But my ten-year-old mind added all those things together and concluded that if I died unbaptized, I was toast!

Despite a godly upbringing in a truly devout home, I cannot truthfully claim that God's love—either his love for me or my love for him—was the conscious motive that moved me to action on that September Sunday morning. What shook me to the core and kicked me in the seat of the pants, the impulse that energized me and dragged me down that aisle to request baptism, was holy terror, raw and naked fear.

Some day my final destination would be either heaven or hell, I was thinking. And the very thought of hell sent chill-bumps racing down my spine. I pushed my way past the people situated between me and the aisle, rushed to the front of the room, and blurted out my request: "I do not want to go to hell. I want God to forgive my sins. I want to be baptized."

Through the years, many sensitive children have been frightened by the fear of hell—just as I was—into receiving Christ as Savior and being baptized. No doubt very many of those children decided later—just as I did—that they really had not made a responsible decision, and so they repeated the conversion experience, "just to be sure." And perhaps some, even after two baptisms, felt the desire (as I later did as a senior in college) to kneel at my bedside and repeat Billy Graham's prayer asking God's forgiveness and inviting Jesus into my heart and life.

When I responded to the invitation song on that September Sunday in 1954, I could not possibly have known that a quarter-century later I would be head-over-heels into a year-long research project on the final fate of the wicked. Nor could I have imagined, on the day I was baptized, that the research project would end with me writing a five-hundred-page book titled *The Fire That Consumes: A Biblical and Historical Study of the Doctrine of Final Punishment.*

I could not have dreamed that the British scholar F. F. Bruce would contribute a foreword to the first edition or that the Evangelical Book Club would choose it as an Alternate Selection. I certainly had no hint in advance that God would use that book to help spark a restudy of the doctrine of hell among Bible-believing Christians on several continents. And I would have laughed with disbelief had anyone dared to suggest in

1954 that my future book would be the subject of a 2012 feature movie titled "Hell and Mr. Fudge," based on the true story behind the book.

Yet it is the sober truth that all these things happened, one after the other, without my planning and certainly apart from my power—which could never have brought any of it into being, much less all of those things. God being sovereign, I trust that each event fell into place according to his agenda, through his power, and to his glory. At most, any of us just happens to be a hunk of mortal clay that he had prepared for some purpose, then picks up and uses when the time is right in his own eyes.

If I am ever tempted to think otherwise, I need only remember that this entire chain of events resulted from an intensive restudy of the subject that *I did not plan,* and required a change of my own mind that *I did not desire.* Indeed, I would have happily avoided the entire matter and everything connected with it, had there been any honest way around it.

But in the end there was not another honest way. Truth is more important than material comfort, my Daddy used to say—and I trusted his opinions more than the opinions of anybody else in the whole world. In fact, it is fair to say that my five siblings and I were raised on just such godly affirmations as that.

2   ENLARGING THE CONVERSATION

While researching the doctrine of final punishment about twenty-five years later, I discovered that many of my childhood ideas about hell were based firmly on the Scriptures and needed no adjustment. Those things deserved to be taught, defended, and perpetuated because they are clearly taught in the Word of God.

These truths are not lifted from their settings and harvested as proof-texts. They are studied in context with due regard to the meanings of words, using the tools and following the rules of standard biblical exegesis (bringing out the sense) and hermeneutics (interpreting the meaning). The picture of hell as it looked in my ten-year-old imagination included some other elements that definitely needed restudy.

At the time, I would have insisted that these details also belonged in the box of items marked "Things-we-know-for-sure." But no matter how strongly I might have insisted—or with what volume or intensity or repetition—I still would have been wrong. However, God is merciful, and he steers us to the light when light is what we are seeking (John 3:16-19).

Part of my assignment for that year-long project was to discover the origin of the doctrine of everlasting conscious torment. As it happened, I found that origin to be in Greek philosophy and not in Holy Scripture. Of course, many others through the centuries had made the same discovery before I did, and I would never claim otherwise.

I will tell you this—with no desire to exaggerate or to be controversial—that no one before or after could have been more *astounded* at the things I found throughout the Bible during the course of my study. I knew instinctively that I had to write a book. Time and again, I prayed for God to give me a spirit of wisdom and of revelation as I opened the Scriptures to another passage (Eph. 1:17). Time and again I was surprised by the truth that stood out in some familiar text, as if I were reading it for the very first time.

In the end, I wrote that book. It was titled *The Fire That Consumes: A Biblical and Historical Study of the Doctrine of Final Punishment,* and I mentioned it briefly in the previous chapter. In *The Fire That Consumes,* I examined every passage of Scripture in both Old and New Testaments that comments on the topic of final punishment.

I *had* to share what I had found with my Christian brothers and sisters. If I had read the Bible correctly, they also deserved to know these things that had surprised me so. And, if my thinking was wrong, someone needed to write a better book than mine, to point that out very plainly for everyone to see.

The book you are reading now is titled *Hell: A Final Word.* That title reminds us that when hell finally has completed its job, there will be nothing left to say. Everyone who goes there will be gone, entirely and eternally. For everyone who continued throughout life in opposition to God, "hell" will have become the "final word."

But the title *Hell: A Final Word* also has a second meaning. Since 1982, I have written two separate books and one major revision on the subject of hell. The book in your hand at this moment will be my last book on that subject. In the final few paragraphs of this chapter, let me fill in a few details about those books as background to this one.

Bringing you current

The Fire That Consumes landed in the world of evangelical Christianity like a match lighting a fuse going straight to a bundle of dynamite. Carefully and kindly, it directly challenged the traditional Christian understanding of hell as a place of unending conscious torment—the "orthodox" view that had been held for at least 1,600 years by almost the entire Christian world. Most important, its challenge to the nearly universal understanding of hell rested solely on the Word of God, the Bible. Because its power is in the Word of God, *The Fire That Consumes* has had a dramatic effect on the larger conversation. One traditionalist author considered it "the start of the current conservative attack on hell."[1]

A second, British edition of *The Fire That Consumes* was published in 1994 by Paternoster Press in the U.K., with a new foreword by the Anglican priest-scholar John W. Wenham of Oxford. For half a century, Mr. Wenham had championed the high authority of Scripture, both within the Anglican Church and among British evangelical Christians in general. He was also, for several decades, the author of the most widely-used Greek textbook published in the English-speaking world. This second edition of *The Fire That Consumes* is no longer in print.

In the year 2000, InterVarsity Press published *Two Views of Hell: A Biblical and Theological Dialogue*, in which I presented the case for conditional immortality or annihilationism, Robert A. Peterson presented the case for everlasting torment (traditionalism), and we each responded to the other. That book, which gives the reader these two views, continues to sell steadily.

In the spring of 2011, Cascade Books, the academic/theological division of Wipf and Stock, released the third edition of *The Fire That Consumes*. Like the two previous editions, it included a new foreword—this time by Richard Bauckham, Emeritus Professor of New Testament at the University of St. Andrews, Scotland, now at Cambridge University in

England. Although Professor Bauckham is not yet so well known among non-scholars in the United States, in academic circles he is regarded as one of the top New Testament scholars in the world today.

As it happens, books written in defense of the traditional view of hell regularly quote Richard Bauckham's description of the extent to which church-going believers have abandoned the traditional view of hell. However, I have not seen one traditionalist author who mentions that Dr. Bauckham himself has rejected the traditional view of hell as unending torment, or that his personal website now includes an article in which he endorses the same view of final punishment that I have set out in this book you are now reading.

The conversation continues

The new third edition of *The Fire That Consumes* was a major revision of the earlier editions, thoroughly reorganized, with several new chapters. But perhaps the most important addition to the third edition was the interaction throughout the book with seventeen leading defenders of the traditionalist view.

During the twenty-nine years between the publication of the first edition of *The Fire That Consumes* in 1982 and the third edition in 2011, these seventeen widely-recognized evangelical scholars had written twelve books in response to my book and others. In the third edition, I replied to their objections and responded to what I considered problems in their defenses of the traditional view. This continued the conversation that began nearly three decades ago.

Hell is a subject that the sixteenth-century Reformers did not reach to restudy. It is a topic still crying out for serious Bible study. The evangelical conversation on hell has been too long coming, and now that it has started, it desperately needs to grow both deeper and broader. This is my goal in writing *Hell: A Final Word*—to put the same biblical data and historical facts into the hands of serious Bible students and readers in general that the scholars have had for at least thirty years.

A best-selling book in 1986 was titled *All I Really Need to Know I Learned in Kindergarten: Uncommon Thoughts on Common Things,* by Robert Fulghum. The title speaks eloquently for itself. Nothing of great importance is new, the author tells us. Things that matter most are mostly obvious.

It is a bit like that with hell. Most of what I thought about hell as a ten-year-old, I continue to believe and teach today. Before we go further, let's pause and pay tribute to the simple truths about hell that always remain—the elements of good theology that need no revising.

3   A PRIMER ON HELL

How can I begin to describe the hell I imagined on my baptismal day in September 1954? Decades of additional Bible study on the topic have only confirmed the accuracy of most of what I already believed at age ten. Thinking back on that scene now, just three years short of birthday number seventy, five brief statements sum up what I already believed about hell so many years ago.

> Hell is real.
> Hell is bad.
> Hell is punishment.
> Hell is separation from God.
> Hell is eternal.

Hell is real

Make no mistake about it—hell is *real*. Despite all the jokes and cartoons, it is as real as heaven. It is real, despite the totally fictitious details invented by Dante and other medieval figures, and by today's flimflam artists and internet sensationalists. Hell is real, despite the crust of human traditions that has accumulated around the true teaching of Scripture until the original version is hardly even recognizable.

When the New Testament refers to "hell" as the place of final punishment, it translates the Greek word *gehenna*. However, there are some who say that the lost are never raised from the dead. They never face God in judgment. They are never expelled into hell based on a judicial sentence of divine justice. In this explanation of things, the lost simply remain dead forever. This view says that *gehenna* refers to the grave alone and to nothing more.

Jesus seems clearly to disallow this viewpoint. When he was sending out his disciples on a mission into dangerous territory at the risk of their lives, Jesus exhorted them not to fear human beings, who could do no more than to kill them now. Instead, Jesus urged his disciples to fear God who, after killing the body, has power to throw people into hell (Luke 12:5), where he is able to destroy both soul and body forever (Matt. 10:28). There is a second death for the wicked. The grave is not their end. Hell is indeed *real.*

Others acknowledge that Jesus warned of *gehenna,* and that he pictured it as a horrible and dreadful destination. They freely admit that Jesus said that God "is able to destroy both soul and body in hell" (Matt. 10:28). But having said that, these deniers insists that God is "too good" to allow anyone actually to go to hell. Why, however, would Jesus warn of something that he knew would never take place? The teachings of Jesus that we have considered already are sufficient to refute this wishful thinking.

Hell is bad

One could argue that it is pointless to say that hell is bad, because everybody knows that already. The final point in that statement is probably accurate. Who is not familiar with the ubiquitous cartoon featuring a red devil with horns and pitchfork, prodding a helpless mortal whom he has been assigned to torment? The internet is full of fanciful fictions about petroleum or gas crews drilling in the remote parts of Siberia or elsewhere, whose seismic instruments supposedly picked up the screams of people in hell, deep in the center of the earth. Society understands that hell is bad.

On the other hand, the notion is widespread that hell will be a picnic in the park for rogues and scoundrels, an eternity of nonstop partying and having a high old time forever with one's earthly friends. This vision of infernal camaraderie might be as mild as Huckleberry Finn's, which author Samuel Clemens reveals in an early conversation Huck has with Miss Watson, the spinster sister of his caretaker Aunt Mollie:

> Then she told me all about the bad place, and I said I wished I was there. She got mad then, but I didn't mean no harm. All I wanted was to go somewhere; all I wanted was a change; I wasn't particular . . . .
>
> Now she had got a start, and she went on and on and told me all about the good place. . . . I asked her if she reckoned Tom Sawyer would go there, and she said not by a considerable sight. I was glad about that, because I wanted him and me to be together.[2]

Make no mistake about it: hell is not a place of laughter—not even the slightly naughty kind. In fact, when Jesus talks about hell, he pictures it as a place of weeping, or a place of defiant anger, but never as a "fun" place, never as a place where anyone is laughing or even smiling just a little.

Hell is punishment

Jesus not only taught that hell is real. He also taught that hell is *punishment.* What comes to your mind when you see or hear the word "punishment"? Could you think of a prisoner who has been confined to a dark and smelly, underground cell, where his only human contact is a jailor who torments the prisoner at every opportunity? Or perhaps the word "punishment" conjures the scene of a man paying a fine to the magistrate.

Or might you visualize an ancient site of executions, where Roman soldiers are viciously scourging ten men? When the scourging is ended, the near-dead men are nailed to crosses, where they will hang until life is gone. These three scenes differ considerably, but what we see in each of them can truthfully be called "punishment."

They are all fairly labeled as "punishment," not because of what each man suffers, or how much he suffers, or how the suffering endured by any particular one compares with the conscious pain experienced by the others. What makes them "punishment" is the fact that each situation we described was the penal consequence of crimes committed, as officially ordered by a judge with authority to pronounce guilt and to pass sentence based on law.

According to Jesus, every human being—wicked and good alike—will be raised from the dead to face God regarding the deeds done in the body now. "A time is coming," Jesus said, "when all who are in their graves will hear [Jesus'] voice and come out—those who have done good . . . to the resurrection of life . . . and those who have done evil . . . to the resurrection of judgment" (John 5:28-29, emphasis added). We can mark it down as settled truth: What happens in hell in the Age to Come will be the consequence of choices, actions and inactions here and now (Mark 9:43-47).

By the way, did you notice that no text we have read about hell even remotely suggests that hell's punishment is a means of instruction, or that it is intended to rehabilitate or restore? As you continue to study the Bible on this topic of final punishment, you will not find a single hint that those who are banished to hell will ever come out again. Nor is there any Scripture that suggests that bad conduct in hell prolongs the punishment, which already is said to be eternal.

Hell is separation from God

In all the teaching of Jesus, no element stands out more vividly than that final judgment will result in two destinations. Hell will involve separation from family and friends, if some are redeemed and some have rejected

God's grace. But far more important, it will mean final separation from God. Not everyone finally goes to heaven.

Jesus describes scenes of a great party, from which some would-be guests are tossed out (Matt. 8:11-12). He tells stories of people expelled into the darkness outside, a place noted for weeping and gnashing of teeth (Matt. 22:13). Another parable describes a fisherman separating the edible good fish from the "trash" fish that are sold as bait (Matt. 13:47-50).

The world of Jesus' parables is a world full of separations: weeds must be separated from grain (Matt. 13:30). And in Jesus' most famous parable of this sort, he compares God's final separation of human beings to the separation of sheep and goats by a Palestinian herdsman (Matt. 25:31-46).

But far more dreadful than human separations is the total separation of the lost person from God the Creator and from Jesus Christ the redeemer. But that is a sober reality and not an idle threat either. Jesus spoke of some to whom he will say in judgment, "Go away from me!" (Matt. 7:23). The Apostle Paul says that when Jesus is revealed from heaven, he will "inflict vengeance" on the wicked. They will "suffer the punishment of eternal destruction and exclusion from the presence of the Lord" (2 Thess. 1:9, RSV).

Hell is eternal

When we come to the subject of last things in the New Testament, nearly everything in sight is marked "eternal." The unknown author of Hebrews refers to "eternal *judgment*" (Heb. 6:2). Jesus speaks of "eternal *punishment*" (Matt. 25:46) and "eternal *fire*" (Matt. 25:41). Paul speaks of "eternal *destruction*" (2 Thess. 1:9). Many texts speak of "eternal *life*" (John 3:16). Although the exact expression "eternal hell" does not appear, there can be no doubt that hell belongs in the category of things that are eternal.

Clearly something about hell is *eternal*. Exactly what that is, and what it means, is the subject of earnest conversation and sometimes heated debate among the scholars.

The traditional majority view says that hell is eternal, that those who go to hell are eternal, and that they will live eternally in hell. In addition, this view says the torments of hell are eternal and will never end. When I was baptized at age ten, that was what I had been taught and so that is what I thought.

Where did the details of that hell originate? Did they come from the Bible? If so, in which Scripture texts can they be found? Did I make up the picture of hell that was so frightening to me that day? Might that picture of hell have been created by some author of great literature? Was it born from the pen of some medieval poet such as Aligieri Dante, author of *The Divine Comedy* (perhaps best known for its first section, *Inferno*)? Did my hell of unending torment that never, never ends perhaps begin with John Milton's famous saga *Paradise Lost?*

Could it be possible that the hell I imagined that day owes its details, not to Scripture at all, but rather to some preacher who replaced the Bible's plain language with his own vision of hell, simply because he thought the Bible's picture of hell was not clear enough?

History is full of imaginative preachers. We have plenty of examples from which to choose all throughout church history. For example, we might look at statements on hell by Chrysostom or Augustine (fifth century), or Wesley or Edwards (eighteenth century), or Spurgeon or Moody (nineteenth century). These men all wrote their sermons, and collections of their sermons are usually accessible today on the internet.

All these preachers took hell very seriously. They believed that the word "punishment" required pain of body and soul, and that such pain would be constant with no intermission. And they believed that the word "eternal" made it necessary for that pain to continue forever without end.

When they spoke of hell, that is what they envisioned, and they worked very hard to communicate that same vision to those who heard them preach or who read their works.

It is enough to say that a Bible full of surprises has led me to a very different conclusion. This is a book about those surprises. Many ideas about hell have developed over the centuries. Did you know, for example, that the worst section of hell in Dante's *Inferno* is not the hottest, but rather is *freezing cold?*

Today it is not enough to ask if someone believes in hell. It is necessary also to ask the nature of the hell in which they believe. If you are not already convinced of that, just talk to some of the folks walking down a street in any city.

4 WHICH HELL DO WE MEAN?

Imagine that a major television network is preparing a special program on popular beliefs concerning the afterlife. You have been hired as a pollster to interview people on the street about hell. These are some opinions you would certainly encounter:

"Hell? I believe heaven and hell are *now*. Heaven is the good stuff we experience in this life and hell is all the bad."

"What do I think about hell? I don't believe in it. A good God would not send anyone to hell."

"Bad people go to hell when they die, where they suffer horrible torment in fire forever."

"What is hell like? It will differ according to each person's own tastes and desires. One person's heaven might be another person's hell."

"I think that hell is the grave. That's all. When wicked people die, that's the end of them. Period."

We've all seen the stereotypical representations of Satan and hell. There's the devil—that red, horned creature with a pointed tail, fiery pitchfork in hand—mercilessly shoving his victims into the pit of hell. And what a pit it is—a murky chasm, rumbling like a hot, bubbling cauldron, belching steam and rancid vapors. From its smoky depths echo the torturous screams of the damned.

From Dante's *Inferno* to late night B movies, our supposedly Christian culture has accepted a view of hell that owes more to human imagination and pagan myth than to the Bible. Unfortunately, the mythology has also invaded many pulpits—even in churches which desire to teach nothing but the Bible, churches led by good pastors who are completely sincere.

Of course, most modern speakers don't present the late-night movie version of hell described above. However, their ancestors in the pulpit did present that overdrawn picture in mythical proportions. Two examples from leading preachers of the nineteenth and twentieth centuries are enough to demonstrate the point.

Consider this quotation from a sermon preached by Charles Spurgeon on September 4, 1855. In this sermon, Spurgeon personalizes his description of a sinner being thrown into hell to include each member of his audience.

> The angel, binding you hand and foot, holds you one single moment over the mouth of the chasm. He bids you look down— down—down. There is no bottom; and you hear coming up from the abyss, sullen moans, and hollow groans, and screams of tortured ghosts. You quiver, your bones melt like wax, and your marrow quakes within you . . . .
>
> Ye shriek and cry, ye beg for mercy; but the angel, with one tremendous grasp, seizes you fast, and then hurls you down, with the cry, "Away, away!" And down you go to the pit that is bottomless, and roll for ever downward—downward—downward—ne'er to find a resting-place for the soles of your feet. Ye shall be cast out.[3]

Early in 2011, I engaged in a friendly debate with a professor at an evangelical college in southern California on the nature of hell. Throughout the debate, he claimed to represent what the church has always taught. Yet before the night was over, the professor was saying that those in hell do not necessarily feel any pain. The good professor was in a bind, squeezed from one side by an intellectual sense of obligation to say what "the church has always taught," but pressed from the emotional side by all that is merciful and humane to minimize the horror of the traditional position.

The professor in California certainly did *not* represent "what the church has always taught" when he denied that the lost feel pain. Charles Spurgeon, from whom we just heard, would roll over in his grave at such an idea! So would A. W. Pink, an influential twentieth-century representative of the traditional view of hell, who wrote the following description of hell's torments: "To help your conception, imagine yourself to be cast into a fiery oven, all of a glowing heat, or into the midst of a blowing brick-kiln, or of a great furnace, where your pain would be as much greater as that occasioned by accidentally touching a coal of fire, as the heat is greater."[4]

And how will the redeemed react to such eternal torment? Will they beg God on behalf of the lost to save them, or even mercifully to allow them to die? Will the saved simply avoid the torture scene and keep it far from mind? Probably so, according to most sensitive Christians you encounter in your survey.

However, those same believers would likely wince in disbelief at the answer of Dr. John H. Gerstner, who claimed to speak for orthodox Reformed Christianity at the end of the twentieth century. Gerstner saw himself continuing the tradition of Jonathan Edwards, insisting that godly people should already find great pleasure in reflecting on the agonies of the damned. Few people would go to such an extreme, but to show just how far some have gone, we hear these incredible words from Dr. Gerstner:

"If [a Christian] loves God, he must love hell, too. If God decrees it, it must be good and for God's glory, and the evangelical knows that he will sing God's praises eternally as the smoke ascends from the burning pit! AMEN! . . . When Christ asks, 'Do you love Me? He is asking also "Do you love hell?"'[5]

And again: "Even *now* while the evangelical is singing the praises of his Lord and Savior, Jesus Christ, he knows that multitudes are suffering the torments of the damned. . . . The true Christian, aware of this, is happily, exuberantly, gladly praising the Judge of the Last Day, Jesus Christ, who has sentenced to such merited damnation millions of souls."[6]

To be sure, most thoughtful Christians today probably reject such teaching. Yet your poll will show that, even in this kinder and gentler age,[7] the majority Christian opinion about hell still raises some troublesome questions—and leaves plenty with which to quarrel. For, according to the majority traditional view, we must believe that God finally will keep millions of people alive forever in a place resembling a fiery furnace. There he will torment them endlessly with some type of pain throughout all eternity.

The mere mention of such a fate deeply stirs anyone who takes the possibility seriously. Such a subject is too important for careless thinking and too awful for uncaring feelings. This is the time for tough minds and tender hearts.

5 TOUGH MINDS AND TENDER HEARTS

Our first question must always be: *"Is this what the Bible teaches?"* How we might *feel* about hell cannot be the measure of what hell really will be. Despite the sensational tales of some who claim to have been there, all that we really know about hell comes from the Bible. We must be very careful to form our own understanding about hell from the sacred pages of Scripture. However, that does not mean that we cannot ask honest questions as we examine widespread notions about hell in light of God's Word.

For example, what does the traditional doctrine tell your mind and heart about the *character of God* whom you love and worship, the same God you sometimes beg in prayer to relieve your own suffering and that of others? Is this picture of hell consistent with the Bible's stories about *Jesus*—whom to see, is to see the Father? Must we believe that God, who made every human being in his own image, and who is sorry when even a sparrow dies, will torment men and women forever—although he could easily allow them to die instead?

Perhaps you have assumed, as I once did, that the Bible requires such a view of hell. After all, everlasting torment is what almost everyone *says* the Bible teaches. But have you never doubted or wondered whether such a picture could be true? Many sensitive Christians have struggled with the traditional doctrine of hell. Supposing that it came from Scripture, however, most of them have suppressed their deepest thoughts and feelings and remained quiet.

Astonishingly, many believers have become so accustomed to the idea that the lost will agonize in conscious torment forever that they scarcely give it a second thought. Indeed, the traditional doctrine of hell as everlasting conscious agony has gained such acceptance during the past sixteen centuries that millions of good-hearted people placidly accept it as necessary to believing the Bible. Yet these same individuals instinctively recoil in horror whenever they hear the news of some temporary human atrocity—whether it be detestable child abuse, a mass murder, or an especially vicious assault or rape.

Others, who have not become desensitized by long familiarity with the traditional doctrine of hell, are appalled. Thousands, perhaps millions, of people created and loved by God have fled from him in horror at the thought that he would torture anyone forever. Famous atheists have attributed their unbelief to this traditional Christian teaching.

For more than half a century, British philosopher Antony Flew was the face and voice of atheism in England. He wrote against God and debated Christians. He tried to destroy faith. Then one day, Antony Flew's logic caught up with him. He had been wrong, he said. There is a supernatural being whose work the universe reflects. But don't think that Antony Flew, the atheist son of a Methodist preacher, is about to become an evangelical Christian, he cautioned. In Flew's opinion, a God who would torment humans forever without end would be unworthy of their worship.

Surely Flew was out of place in deciding what God must be like in order to deserve worship. But the traditional view of final punishment as everlasting conscious torment ought not to stop anyone from being a believer in God, Jesus Christ, the gospel, or the Bible. Scripture nowhere suggests that God is an eternal tormenter. It never says the damned will writhe in ceaseless pains, or that the glories of heaven will forever be blighted by the screams from hell. The Bible does not teach the traditional doctrine of everlasting conscious torment. Don't blame God for something he never really said.

Today, devout believers in increasing numbers are saying aloud what they have long believed—that the doctrine of everlasting torment slanders God's character as revealed in the Bible and in the life of Jesus Christ. By challenging the basis of the traditional hell, a person nobly imitates the ancient Bereans, whom Luke commended for testing a teaching by searching the Scriptures to see if it was so (Acts 17:10-11).

These are not rebellious people on the fringe of Christianity. They are faithful workers, humble disciples, who are prayerfully devouring God's word to digest whatever it has to say. Asking questions is an act of extraordinary courage. It is not easy to challenge a belief that almost everyone holds—and has held for at least 1,600 years.

Can you consider it possible that the majority interpretation of hell as conscious everlasting torment is *not* the teaching of Scripture after all? That is a very important question, because the Bible is our final authority. Whatever it teaches is right, no matter what any person may say. So I ask it again. Does the Bible *really teach* that God finally will keep people alive forever in hell just to suffer torment that never ends? Does Scripture *require* us to believe that will be the destiny of *most* men and women whom God loved and sent his Son to redeem? If that is *not* what Scripture teaches, is it not a *slander* against the heavenly Father almost too heinous to describe?

Suppose for the moment that I am quoting God accurately in saying that human beings who reject his grace will finally be cut off from his life-giving Presence and cease to exist. How do you think it makes God feel for someone to misquote him by saying that he will keep wrongdoers alive forever in hell and torment them without end?

Imagine your reaction in a roughly similar situation. Suppose you hired a babysitter for your evening out. You learn later that she told your children *that you said* you would punish any misbehavior by putting staples in their fingers, cutting off their ears, then stuffing them into the microwave oven until they popped. And suppose your children were young enough that such nonsense made them question and distrust your parental love.

If you are like me, there would be no words strong enough to describe your feelings in response. Yet the babysitter's misrepresentation is nothing by comparison with the slander against God, if everlasting torment is not true.

Some express concern that without the threat of everlasting torment, sinners will lose all motivation to repent. There is no cause for alarm. God's judgment remains severe but it is also fair. Those who go to hell will suffer conscious pain exactly measured by perfect, holy, divine justice. The ultimate punishment common to all the lost will become a reality: they will *cease to be*. From Genesis to Revelation, the Bible repeatedly warns that the wicked will "die," "perish" or be "destroyed."

In John's vision in Revelation, a voice from the Throne refers to this punishment as the "second death" (Rev.21:8). This is capital punishment of an infinite sort. It destroys both soul and body . . . forever. It is no wonder that Jesus refers to it as *eternal* punishment (Matt. 25:46), or that Paul calls it *eternal* destruction (2 Thess. 1:9). This death-punishment is indeed "eternal." Those who die this second death will never live again.

But another question also looms in the background like the dark clouds of an approaching storm. Whatever we finally understand hell to be—whether unending torment or total annihilation—must we suppose that most of the human race will go there in the end?

6   WHO GOES TO HELL?

It is frequently stated that Jesus says more about hell than anyone else in the Bible. Unfortunately, when anyone says only that much—that Jesus says more about hell than anyone else—the result is often a miscommunication.

This happens whenever someone hears the word "hell," but thinks "unending torment," then concludes that Jesus says much about unending torment. In fact, Jesus never mentions unending torment, and what he says about hell explains why he does not.

Jesus uses the word "hell" (*gehenna*) eleven times and is the only person in the Bible who uses it at all to speak of final punishment. It is important to know *what* Jesus says about hell.

Hell is the place, Jesus warns, where God is able to *destroy* both soul and body (Matt. 10:28). The same verse says that this destruction is total and includes the whole person, soul and body alike. On another occasion, Jesus repeats the description of the destructive process found in Isaiah 66:24 and applies it to *gehenna*. The most obvious details in that text are the worms that do not die, in fires that cannot be extinguished (Mark 9:43-48). Such irresistible fire and maggots will consume corpses until nothing remains. Since the whole being is totally destroyed, everlasting torment is out of the question.

It is also instructive to notice whom Jesus addresses about hell, and who he says will go there. Strikingly, he does *not* address his remarks on hell to the riff-raff, prostitutes, drunkards, or tax collectors—the people who traditionally were recipients of "hell-fire" preaching by the rabbis at that time. Instead, Jesus' remarks about hell are almost always directed either to his own disciples or to the religious leaders of Israel. In the Gospels, Jesus normally does not talk about hell to public crowds, and he never singles out the "sinners" in particular.

On the question of who is going to hell, Jesus differs again from most teachers of his time—and of ours. He warns the person who verbally abuses a fellow human (Matt. 5:22). He cautions the man whose eye leads him to sin (Matt. 5:29-30). He describes the sectarian missionary who makes proselytes—then makes them twice as bad as himself (Matt. 23:15). And, although Jesus does not use the word "hell" *(gehenna)* in the story, that is clearly the fire into which he says people will go who see others suffering and turn the other way (Matt. 25:31-46).

As a lad, growing up Christian in a small Southern town, I knew some believers who took all matters of true religion extremely seriously. And if anyone ever asked who will go to hell, these folks were ready and able to answer.

First, all non-Christians, of course—without exception. Jesus is the only way to heaven. Then all the professing Christians who landed in the wrong church. Jesus built *his* church; *people* built the others. Now add all those in the *true* church who are either unsound in doctrine or have erred in practice. Finally, list any of those still left whom God sees as lacking in sincerity, commitment, or genuine repentance.

Some days it seems everybody will go to hell. Other days offer hope for a few exceptional saints to miss it and be saved. Barely, of course. But is that the approach of Scripture? Does this analysis sound like Jesus? Is it harmonious with the spirit of the gospel? I must confess that there were times in my younger life when the caricature above would have been a picture of me, with my rationalized self-righteousness and easy condemnation of others.

Boy, was I wrong! Misguided. Not seeing the forest for the trees. I have had to ask God for forgiveness. And sometimes, when I have encountered people whom I knew and judged in those days, I have had to ask their forgiveness also. What a mess I made. But as my friend Jeff Walling says, if there were no *mess* we would not need a *Mess*-iah!

Some biblical points about salvation

So who will go to hell? More than a handful of people, to be sure. Yet Scripture is not nearly so stingy in its expectations on this point as many of us are. Let's consider some of the Bible's statements that might cause one to think otherwise.

There is no salvation in any name except the name of Jesus (Acts 4:12). That wonderful affirmation highlights the uniqueness of Jesus Christ and of the saving work he has accomplished for sinners. It tells us that every person in the new heavens and earth will owe it all to Jesus. It constantly reminds us that the only hope for sinners rests in the atoning work of Jesus Christ, symbolized by his life, death, and resurrection.

To affirm this ancient Christian confession is to deny that there are many paths to God, of which Jesus Christ is one. That idea is called "pluralism." It is increasingly popular in a society that believes all truth is subjective and that no truth is any more "true" than another truth, even one that says the opposite of the first.

Salvation is ours by grace through faith (Eph. 2:8-9). This means it is undeserved and not deserved. It is received and not earned. Because it is a gift, we must be content to trust God for it.

The same principles apply to everyone. God rescues all human beings. It does not matter if one is a Jew or a Gentile . . . or where one lives . . . or when one lives. God declared Abraham in the right with himself ("justi-fied" him) based on Abraham's faith-trust in God's promise to Abraham.

Significantly, this took place *before* Abraham was circumcised. The timing is important, says Paul, for it shows clearly that God declares *all people* in the right based on their trust-faith in God's promises, whether they are Jew or Gentile (Rom. 4:10-12).

God will judge each person based on the light from God that person pos-sessed. He will not judge people based on light they did not have and could not have obtained (John 3:20-21). We have seen that Abraham was declared right with God through his trust-faith in God's promise *that he knew* (Rom. 4:19-22). Today, God normally encounters people in a saving way through the gospel. However, God is able to accomplish his plans by making stones cry out if he sees fit (Luke 19:40).

We are forbidden to pass judgment on other people (Matt. 7:1). There are several good reasons for this very wise prohibition. We do not know their opportunities or their circumstances. And we cannot see the heart. We are also incapable of passing judgment on others because we cannot carry out the sentence—whether it be to save or to destroy (James 4:13).

We can read about the many and the few in the perspective of God's wishes. Jesus speaks of "many" on the roadway to destruction, and "few" that find the path to life (Matt. 7:13-14). When we are talking about a God who does not wish for *any* to perish (2 Pet. 3:9) but for *all* to be saved (1 Tim. 2:4), even one person finally lost is too *many.*

The beginning promise of the Bible's salvation story encourages us to be very optimistic. This is true whether we think of relative numbers or rela-tive percentages of saved and lost. The story opens with Abram, to whom God comes with something new. Not a law to keep. Not a deal to take advantage of. Not an opportunity to exploit. God comes with a promise—a promise for Abraham to trust, and lean on, and live by—a promise for

God to fulfill. Abraham's spiritual descendants will be as numerous as the stars in the sky, as many as the sands by the seashore (Gen. 22:17).

The near-closing vision of the Bible's salvation story encourages us to be very optimistic. As the story nears its end, John sees in a vision a multitude of men and women from every political, ethnic, and linguistic category. They are celebrating victory by the blood of the Lamb. This multitude is so huge it cannot be counted (Rev. 7:1-12).

God is predisposed to save, not to condemn. We have it from Jesus himself. God sent the Son into the world to *save* the world, not to *condemn* the world (John 3:17). It seems that human beings are programmed, whether by genetics, environment, or habitual choices and conduct, to see the good in any situation and be hopeful, or to notice the bad and to fall into despair. Stated in those terms, God is always leaning toward saving people and not condemning them.

Some things that are not reasons anyone goes to hell

Based on the gospel itself and the New Testament's explanations, implications, and applications of the gospel, we can identify some things that are *not* reasons anyone will go to hell.

No one will go to hell because God made them go. There is a form of Calvinism which says that before creation, God programmed everything that would ever happen, then sat back to watch the show. In this view of matters, the final destiny of every individual was settled before any human existed, whether heaven or hell, and there is simply nothing anyone can do to change that.

I have studied and struggled for forty-five years with the issues that divide Calvinists from non-Calvinists and I have no brilliant plan for reconciliation. Scripture clearly says that we call on God for salvation, but that he called us long before that (Acts 2:21, 38). That statement, it seems to me, is no more or less shocking than the statement that we love God because he loved us first (1 John 4:19). I tend to approach such situations with a desire to collect all the good I can from both sides, and have learned to live with unanswered questions.

The bottom line, by my calculation, is that the saved must give God all the credit for their salvation, while for their condemnation the unsaved must take all the blame. We see this illustrated in Luke's account of Paul's second Sabbath sermon in the Jewish synagogue in Antioch of Pisidia. The message draws a mixed response: some contradict and some believe (Acts 13:45-48). Luke notes that "as many as were *ordained to eternal life* believed" (the saved give God the credit). But Paul tells the opponents that they *judge themselves* "unworthy of eternal life" (the condemned take all the blame). The two "sides" of this scenario (saved vs. lost) are simply not symmetrical.

Similarly, John 3 records Jesus' comments about those who receive eternal life (v. 16) and also about those who are condemned and perish (v. 18). It is surely significant that Jesus blames the condemned person for his own condemnation ("*because* he has not believed"), but when he describes the person who receives eternal life, there is no human *because*.

No one will go to hell based solely on Adam's sin. We suffer many consequences from Adam's sin as our representative, and if Jesus had not come, we all would have gone to hell because of Adam's sin. But Jesus *did* come—also as our representative—and the consequences of his obedience "much more" than outweigh all the consequences of Adam's sin (Rom. 5:12-21).

No one will go to hell merely because he or she was born in a particular time or place and not in another. God will judge based on available light, and a person either loves or hates light whatever its content and wherever its location (Acts 10:34-35).

No one will go to hell because of "missing" the true church. There have been "true" churches that imagined themselves superior to others ever since some believers at Corinth adopted the slogan that said, "We are of Christ." All churches claiming that they alone are "the true church" have at least this much in common: they all are wrong in making that claim.

As many faults, errors, sins, and problems as the Corinthian church had, Paul addressed them as "the church of God that is in Corinth" (1 Cor. 1:2). His confidence for them was based on *God's* actions: his calling, his grace, his gifting, his confirming, and demonstrations of his divine faithfulness (1 Cor. 1:2-9). Like Paul, our hope is to be found "in Christ," not in any "true church" or particular segment of his always-imperfect followers (Phil. 3:8-9).

No one will go to hell for accidentally misunderstanding some doctrinal point while sincerely seeking God's will. If there ever was an important issue in the church, surely the truth that there is only one God and one Lord would qualify (1 Cor. 8:1-3). Apparently some at Corinth were confused about even that. Paul's response: "It's not what you know that finally counts, but who knows you." This does not mean that Paul considered the subject of little importance. He wrote the letter we call First Corinthians, among other reasons, to correct the mistaken thinking on this point.

Those who finally go to hell are those who refuse to be saved

Those who go to hell respond to God's grace in a way directly opposite the way believers respond, and the opposite of belief is not unbelief but disbelief (Mark 16:15-16). They intentionally *refuse* to believe. They decide *not* to believe. And they live by the spirit of disbelief all of their life on earth. In the end, God gives them what they had always wanted—never to see, to hear, or to be reminded of God again.

It is not difficult to imagine an adult with such a heart. Most of us have known such a person. What is harder to imagine is a child with that kind of heart. Could a boy of fourteen, for example, ever be so sinful that he would deserve to be kept alive forever for the sole purpose of being tormented without end?

7 WILL DAVY BURN FOREVER?

He was a polite and decent kid, my classmate Davy,[8] and at age fourteen, certainly too young to die. As adults, we know very well that youth does not really bestow invincibility and that the young die too.

Of course, in much of the world babies die every day and mothers expect to bury many of their own offspring. Our very expectation of children outliving the parents is based on the fact that we are so very blessed. But we imagine that we all will live to grow up, and when we are Davy's age, no argument can convince us otherwise.

At fourteen, Davy was too young to drive on a public highway in Alabama, but like most youngsters then and there, he sometimes took the family pickup truck on short outings anyway. This particular evening Davy was alone. That means, of course, that the official fatality report was based entirely on the police investigation, including the accident reconstruction, not on eyewitness testimony.

There were no skid marks, usually meaning no application of brakes. The extent to which the pickup was wrapped around the tree suggested the truck's speed on impact. When all the evidence was spread out and reviewed together, the known facts supported the investigator's conclusion that when the highway made a half U-turn, the truck kept traveling straight ahead, directly into the giant oak that stood there long before the highway had been built. Officially, those were the details that mattered. To Davy's mother, sister, and friends, only one thing mattered. Davy was dead.

So far as I knew, Davy had never received Jesus Christ as Savior (John 1:12-13). Perhaps he was too young to be responsible for sins—some of the preachers talk about an "age of accountability" in that regard. I cannot find that expression in the Bible, but I am far from infallible and might have missed it.

God alone knows Davy's state for sure, and God is the judge of all such things. Without claiming certain knowledge on the subject, I *thought* that Davy had died unforgiven. My own feelings sprang from that belief. I felt sadness first, of course, at his death. That was an immediate feeling that stayed for some time.

Other reactions came more slowly and somewhat later. Why did God let Davy die so young? Did God make him die? Could God have kept Davy from dying? Not, did God have enough power for that, but did God's own rules allow it? Are we all born with a death date already set? If so, is there anything we can do to change it?

But the most troubling questions inquired beyond this life, this death, this grave. Questions that interrupted the mind when it was occupied with matters wholly unrelated to sin and fourteen-year-olds. Questions concerning guilt, and goodness, and God.

We have questions about a God who himself is wholly good, whose character defines guilt for others, and who keeps a record of their sins. Those kinds of questions don't require a friend's death for them to show up, but when a friend like Davy does die, and so young at that, such questions seem to have been waiting just around the corner.

Were the sins of a generally clean-living fourteen-year-old boy bad enough for him to go to hell and burn forever?[9] Suppose Davy had even begun committing some hell-sin every day of his life when he was six years old and he lived to be fourteen. That would be fewer than three thousand sins. And suppose God decreed that everybody burns one year for each unforgiven sin. That would mean Davy had to burn for three thousand years, which is the time covered from King David of Israel until the present. Even if God set the punishment at a thousand years of burning for each sin, Davy would pay his penalty in three million years. And while that is impossible to really imagine, it would at least have an end.

But we have not yet even begun to imagine the hell that we have always been taught, a fire that torments those in it forever. How does anyone begin to visualize that? Maybe it would go something like this.

Imagine an earth made of solid granite, a sphere of rock about 7,900 miles through. Now imagine that one time every million years, a tiny hummingbird flies past and brushes that earth with a feathered wing. How many times would the feathers have to brush against the stone planet to wear away one inch of rock? Are there enough zeros to say how many once-every-million-years brushes it would take to cut that rock earth in half? Yet that much time would be a speck too tiny to see compared to "forever."

Is anyone genuinely surprised that millions who hear the gospel and feel themselves drawn by God's love and by the beautiful character of Jesus Christ, finally dismiss the entire story because what started as good news of eternal life somehow changed into what these hearers perceive as a horror chamber called "hell"?

Is there any wonder that noted atheists from Bertrand Russell[10] to Antony Flew[11] identified the traditional Christian doctrine of hell as a primary reason for disbelief in God and in Jesus Christ? Can anyone be surprised that when devout Christian believers hear the biblical evidence that the lost will finally die, perish, and be destroyed forever, one of the most common, almost-instinctive verbal reactions is something like "That certainly sounds more like God!"

In short, the doctrine of everlasting conscious torment strikes countless numbers of people, ranging from devout believers to militant atheists, as intuitively and irreconcilably inconsistent with fundamental justice and morality.

Again I emphasize that this fact alone does not prove everlasting torment wrong. If every human who ever lived declared the traditional view of hell both immoral and unjust, their unanimous negative reaction would not be reason enough to abandon the doctrine. The only legitimate measure of its truthfulness or falsity is the testimony of Scripture on the subject.

However, if a careful study of the Word of God shows the traditional teaching to be wrong, *or* if Scripture teaches something else to be the final wages of sin, *or*, very significantly, if *both* the above should occur, the apparently widespread aversion to the doctrine of everlasting torment as inherently unfair and unjust suddenly becomes important indeed.

"Ah," say some, "but there's the rub. Who are *you* to talk to God about justice? In fact, how can fallen humans even know what justice looks like when they see it?"

8 CAN WE EVEN TALK ABOUT JUSTICE?

Is it ever right for human beings to consider whether God's judgments are just? Can we even comprehend what "justice" really looks like? Can sinful humans distinguish between fairness and unfairness when we see it? According to the Bible, the answers to these questions are *Yes, Yes* and *Yes*. Or, to be precise, perhaps we should say *Yes, but*.

Both the Old and the New Testament invite us to reflect on God's justice. Throughout Scripture, God reminds us that we can recognize what is just, what is unjust, and that we can confidently tell the difference between the two.

Israel's legal system

When God gave Israel the Law of Moses on Mount Sinai, he defined a society in covenant with himself, with all the complexities that any society involves. Among the details in that Law are provisions for a legal system—including the various areas of law familiar to us today. There are regulations involving commerce, property, and domestic affairs. There are laws concerning governance, public health, and safety. We find law embodied in statutes and in what we call common law. God provided what Israel needed to know for all aspects of their life as his covenant people residing on his land.

To this end, God also provided a judicial system for deciding legal disputes and for implementing his laws. These provisions included judges to carry out both civil and criminal law. When he gave these laws, God specifically identified justice as the goal, and he commanded the judges to practice fairness and to reach just results. "Do no injustice in judgment," he said. "You shall not be partial to the poor or favor the great, but judge your neighbor in righteousness" (Lev. 19:15).

Later, God reminds the people of these same principles. "I charged your judges at that time, 'Hear cases between your brothers, and judge righteously between a man and his brother or the foreigner who is with him'" (Deut. 1:16). Since God tells the people to judge righteously, it is clear that he expects them to know the difference between judgment that is fair and judgment that is unfair.

Abraham pleads for Sodom

Long before the Exodus and the giving of the Law at Sinai, we see indications that God has given human beings the ability to sense and to appreciate that God's activity is just (according to justice) and right (morally "righteous"). When God decides to destroy Sodom and Gomorrah, he sends angels who tell Abraham of his plans in advance. In the beginning of the conversation, God says the destruction is inevitable.

Abraham intercedes for the people of Sodom and begins to bargain with God. In the end, God concedes to Abraham's pleading and agrees to spare the city if ten righteous people can be found. Of course, even that proves to be an unrealistic burden and the city is destroyed. How, one might ask, could a mortal man begin to reason with the Creator to show mercy?

For Abraham, the answer seems obvious—he raises the issue of justice. He puts God on the spot, as it were. "Far be it from You to slay the righteous with the wicked," Abraham says to God, "so that the righteous fare as the wicked! Far be that from You! Shall the Judge of all the earth not do what is right?" (Gen. 18:25.)

Do you see Abraham's argument? God is judge of the whole earth. As such, he always does what is right. It would be unfair—unjust—unrighteous (in this context, these three words all mean the same) for the same fate to befall righteous and wicked people alike. And because of these premises, the only outcome consistent with God's own nature is for him to agree to spare the righteous people in Sodom.

God does whatever he wishes

But cannot God—simply because he is *God*—do whatever he wishes, whether we think it fair or not? The only appropriate answer to that question is a resounding "Yes!" God is in the heavens, and he does exactly as he pleases (Psalm 115:3).

This truth is one that faithful Job learned the hard way—through a long and grievous period of physical suffering, economic disaster, and personal loss. Throughout Job's ordeal, his so-called friends accused him of secret sin so great that it could explain and justify his suffering. Equally insistent, Job asserted his innocence, and challenged God to come down and defend the injustice heaped on him.

In the end of the book, God does finally speak. He reprimands Job's friends, tells them they did not know what they were talking about, and instructs them to ask Job to offer a sacrifice on their behalf. God reminds Job that God is God and Job is not. He restores Job's lost blessings but he does not explain why he allowed them to be lost to begin with. Job says, in summary, "Well, shut my mouth!" and then he does just that.

God is God, the story of Job tells us. Nothing ever changes that. And God is not answerable to his creation—including human beings who have a beef against God, who believe that God has given them a raw deal, who complain that God is unjust. That is one side of the double-sided truth we are now considering.

In Romans 9-11 in the New Testament, the Apostle Paul makes the same point, this time involving ultimate salvation—heaven and hell, if you please. And when he has asked the most difficult of questions, and affirmed the hardest truths, Paul concludes much as the book of Job does. God is God, Paul says. He needs no help from anyone else. He made everything, he controls and sustains the universe, and history will end exactly when God has determined. In view of such truths, the best thing we can say is "Amen."

Along the way, in Romans 9, Paul stretches his point to the most extreme stretching point imaginable. Because God is God, the apostle reasons, he can do anything he wishes—just as a ceramics teacher can make anything he or she wishes from the lump of clay. What is more, Paul says, because humans are creatures made from God's lump of clay, they have no right to object to anything that God wishes to make of them.

This means that, if God should wish to do so, he could create people for the express purpose of destroying them—for any reason that suited him, or for no reason at all—and no human would have any right to complain or to call God into question.

But note carefully that Paul does not say that God actually *did* such a thing. In fact, other passages of Scripture make it very plain that God did *not* do that. But until we acknowledge that God *could* have done so if he wished, we are not in the proper position as creatures to say that is not what God chose to do. Like Job, we must confess that God is God and we are not.

Having said that, we can confidently ask with faithful Abraham, "Will not the judge of all the earth do right?" Because it is God of whom we speak, we know that he will do what is right and just and true.

When Paul addressed the Greeks in Athens, he was speaking to people whose culture had long celebrated justice as an ideal. Paul did not tell them that the concept of judging fairly was beyond their ability to understand. He said that God has appointed a day in which he will judge the world *in righteousness*. God's judgment will be *just* (Acts 17:30-31). In saying that, the apostle expected the Greeks to relate to the concept of justice, to recognize it in practice, and to honor it as a noble ideal.

9 A NERDY KID AND HIS COURSES

Edward Benjamin Fudge was born in North Alabama one year before the end of the Civil War. He grew up during Reconstruction and survived, as they say, "by the hardest." Which meant, in his case, that he married late, lived into his eighties, and left eight children. Benjamin Lee Fudge, the oldest of the eight, was my father.

My grandmother taught my grandfather to read and write, which enabled him in later years to run a country store in addition to dirt farming as a sharecropper on other people's farms. When grandpa was disabled at age sixty-six, my daddy, at sixteen the oldest child, assumed responsibility of providing for the family.

So the four brothers took turns going to school and farming. Daddy read his Bible while the mules rested from plowing rows. Sometimes he practiced delivering his sermons by preaching to the silent fields of cornstalks and tree stumps. At age twenty-one, he went to Nashville to attend David Lipscomb College, then on to Texas to finish a degree in New Testament Greek at Abilene Christian College. He took Bible study very seriously, as part of a personal relationship between him and his Savior.

By the time I was born in 1944, Daddy was preaching every Sunday, although he never relied on preaching for his livelihood. He earned that in his other ministry of publishing and selling Christian books and Bible study materials. Although quite conservative in his opinions, he was broad in his attitude toward other people, whether they agreed with his conclusions or not.

I often thought when growing up, and even now still do, that the primary difference between religious teachers is not the views they hold but whether they genuinely desire to understand Scripture in order to teach and to be shaped by it, or if they simply use Scripture as a means to advance their own career and personal interests.

Daddy did what he professed . . . and perhaps above all else, he taught me and his five younger children to do the same. But sometimes even good intentions are not enough to remove blind spots in understanding, or to open doors that have been shut by common tradition for many, many centuries.

Like many boys growing up, I always wanted to be like my father. For about thirty years, Daddy had a fifteen-minute radio program every Monday through Friday, on which he answered questions that his listeners mailed in concerning Bible passages and Christian living. The program was called "Spiritual Guidance," and I often accompanied my father to the radio station, where I sat quietly across the desk from him as he spoke.

Inspired and encouraged by my father's example, I was always a voracious reader and an independent thinker. For several years as a teenager, I studied religious/spiritual correspondence courses from a wide variety of sources—Christian and non-Christian alike. At one time, I studied material from the Order of the Rose (Rosicrucians), the Knights of Columbus (Roman Catholic), Back to the Bible (evangelical mainstream), Worldwide Church of God (Herbert W. Armstrong), the Voice of Prophecy (Seventh-day Adventist), and Churches of Christ (our own fellowship).

Daddy was always present but never imposing as I read, replied, and often argued with the variety of viewpoints these studies included.

If I had a question, he was available and always willing to provide guidance as requested. In due course the Voice of Prophecy materials came to the subject of final punishment. As far as I can remember, this was my first introduction to any interpretation of hell other than everlasting conscious torment. I was sixteen years old, newly licensed to drive, and learning to steer my way through doctrinal disputes of all kinds.

The particular lesson in this correspondence course pointed to well-known Scripture texts that I had memorized years before. These were verses like Romans 6:23 which says: "For the wages of sin is death, but the free gift of God is eternal life, through Jesus Christ our Lord." Or John 3:16, with its declaration that "God so loved the world that he gave his only-begotten Son, that whosoever believeth in him should not perish but have everlasting life."

The choice is simple and straightforward, the correspondence course pointed out. It is *life* or *death; life* or *perish*. What could possibly be easier to understand? Yet I did not then understand. From this vantage point today, nearly six decades later, I can think of several possible reasons why.

Perhaps I was looking for something more complicated and this answer seemed too simple. It is possible that I did not really hear because what I heard was new to me and I was wishing to hear something old. Is it even possible, I ask myself now, that subconsciously I was unwilling to hear because I did not want to be associated in anyone's mind with the Seventh-day Adventists who produced the Voice of Prophecy course?

In theory, that should be totally irrelevant. Why should it matter for even one second who believes a particular teaching? Truth does not depend on who believes it or how many people accept it. We all say that, but we sometimes forget to practice it.

The only question that counts, the only one worthy of consideration, should be, "What does the Bible say?" This has nothing to do with Roman Catholics or Seventh-day Adventists or Herbert W. Armstrong.

It's a matter of Bible study and that is all. Sounds noble, doesn't it? But it is easier said than done.

My conscious desire was only to know God's truth. I thought my mind was open to receive whatever Scripture taught. But for whatever reason—something I cannot decipher now—on this subject there was a blind spot in my spiritual vision. The blind spot did not affect me alone. It reached beyond me, my household, and my family. This particular blind spot was not limited to my church. It was and is found in almost every denomination or group of identifiable believers today.

In the somewhat fictionalized movie "Hell and Mr. Fudge," there is a scene in which a friend named Arvid McGuire is advising me about the consequences of going against the view of hell that has been taught by almost everyone for at least 1,600 years. In a powerful bit of oral interpretation, accompanied by a two-handed gesture for emphasis, actor Frank Hoyt Taylor says: "Folks are partial to the truth that they a-l-r-e-a-d-y got." So far as I remember, Arvid never really said those words. But he would have spoken the truth if he had.

10 EXCITING TO WALK BY FAITH

My years seemed to pass quickly from childhood to adulthood. Markers came and went—high school graduation . . . college graduation . . . marriage . . . graduate school . . . serving a church. Everything was according to plan. Next on my agenda was gradually to earn a doctorate, then spend a career somewhere teaching Greek and the Bible.

Human plans are predictable, but God's are anything but. Homer Hailey, one of my favorite Bible teachers during eighteen years of Christian education, had a saying: "It's an *exciting* thing to walk by faith!" And as everyone who walks by faith can agree, it also frequently means a life filled with surprises. We cannot imagine in advance God's plans or his power to carry them out (Eph. 3:20). We are mostly along for the ride.

It was February 1972. We lived in St. Louis, Sara Faye and I, and we loved it. I was the preacher at Kirkwood Church of Christ; she taught Senior English at Kirkwood High School. We had met at Florida College as sophomores in 1964. We had quickly discovered that her home town of Franklin, Tennessee was only eighty miles north of my home town of Athens, Alabama. I had grown up making business trips with my dad to Nashville, driving within a hundred yards of her house—but we went 650 and 750 miles away to college to meet as sophomores.

After one year together, Sara Faye transferred to Peabody College (now part of Vanderbilt University) to study English and education. I stayed a third year at Florida College to study Bible under Homer Hailey, then transferred to Abilene Christian College (now University). After one year apart, we both graduated in May 1967, married in June, and moved to Abilene in August. There she taught school while I earned a master's degree in biblical languages, and we moved to St. Louis in the summer of 1968.

Saint Louis University offered a Ph.D. in biblical languages and literature, and I had done a year's worth of prerequisites at Covenant and Eden seminaries, both local institutions. Saint Louis University, here I come! But the phone call came first.

It was my next brother Henry, calling to tell me that our daddy had died at age fifty-seven, unexpectedly, after one week's illness. His sudden, unplanned departure left Mother with the family's Christian publishing company and retail bookstore, three children still at home, and a mountain of debt.

As oldest of six children, my next move seemed obvious. We resigned our jobs in St. Louis, waved goodbye to SLU before we got to say hello, and moved to Athens, Alabama, county seat of Limestone County and "home" to the Fudges since 1805. We built our first house, prepared for the birth of our first child, and struggled to live on one spouse's income for the first time. I took a preaching appointment at a sleepy country church and went to work for my mother in the family publishing business. Each job paid the princely sum of $80 per week.

Mother's elderly parents were life-long missionaries in Africa, where she was born and raised. After Daddy's death, Mother wanted to rejoin her parents. When a group of twenty businessmen who were affiliated with our same religious fellowship presented her with a buy-out offer for the family business, she was ready to sell. One condition was that the jobs of all present employees were safe.

As a very minor part of my job, I was named associate editor of a religious periodical my father had recently acquired. He hoped to rehabilitate it from a contentious history and transform it into a positive instrument of spiritual health.

Our periodical was under long-term attack by another publication that saw itself as savior of the faithful segment of the true church on earth, which just happened to be the same as their constituency. And one of the primary threats requiring this magazine's existence was *me*. My supposed error they named "the grace—unity—fellowship heresy."

I taught that we are not saved on the basis of our own performance records or doctrinal test scores, but by trusting in Jesus who took our place in his life, death, and resurrection; that we are one in Christ with all others who also trust in Jesus; and that we can and should express that unity by joint efforts in good works that all can do in good conscience. They denied all these convictions and denounced me as hell-bound.

When the same group aimed their guns at my old professor Homer Hailey for some supposed error, he would not dignify the attack with a reply, explaining that he didn't mind being swallowed by a whale for his beliefs, but he refused to be nibbled to death by minnows. The image came to my mind more than once.

As the shock waves from these changes gradually settled down, life gained a largely pleasurable routine that often could be called exciting. It must have seemed to God that it was time for more surprises.

11 THE BOTTOM FALLS OUT

On July 10, 1975, I was conducting some business at the printing shop in a nearby town when the telephone rang for me. It was Mother's secretary.

Unknown to us, the men who had bought the family business from Mother had sold it to a nonprofit foundation that published the religious magazine devoted to saving the church. The magazine's publisher and editor had just arrived at our offices to announce the change and to take over as new owners.

I returned to the office immediately. The publisher assured me of his good intentions, and said that his financial backer in California was prepared to provide for my family's future—*if* only I would publicly renounce my teaching on grace, unity, and fellowship. I told him that my convictions resulted from prayerful Bible study and were not for sale.

Within five minutes I was fired, and went home several hours early. In my pockets were paychecks for that week and for two weeks of earned vacation. My wife had recently come home from the hospital with Jeremy, our newborn son. He was fifteen days old that day.

For the next year, God provided our necessities day by day, eventually providing me a job as typesetter in the printing shop our business had used for many years. My wages were $7.00 per hour—almost double my income at the family business and church combined. As a bonus, the owners of the printing shop could not care less about my spiritual beliefs.

About this same time, the elders of the church I served asked to meet with me, the only such request in our entire relationship. They announced that they were dismissing me, and gave two reasons. The longest preacher tenure before me had been two years, and I had been there four. And some church members had concluded from my sermons that I thought people in other denominations might also go to heaven.

A third matter went unstated but had not been unnoticed at the time. I had recently invited a Black brother preacher to lead prayer when he visited our revival, which infuriated an influential man in our congregation. When I learned that he was stirring up trouble over the matter, I confronted him publicly and rebuked his attitude.

For about a year, a group of friends from different churches had been meeting at our home one night each week for Bible reading, worship, and fellowship. Now that I had no preaching responsibilities, we decided to begin meeting as a nondenominational church. Soon a sign appeared on a renovated red barn: "Elm Street Church: A Meeting Place for Christians."

For six years, I was the little church's unofficial and unpaid pastor. We were free in Christ. I was in a place of absolute liberty under the Word, answerable only to godly brothers and sisters with the same allegiance. Out of the recent storms, God had created a safe haven—as if he knew I was about to need one. Life was truly exciting! I did not know it, but another surprise was about to arrive.

12   AN OFFER TOO GOOD TO REFUSE

We had been "churching" in the Barn for three or four years when I received a letter one day from an Australian theologian named Robert D. Brinsmead. Brinsmead was publisher, editor, and primary writer of *Verdict Magazine*, a journal focused on the Reformation and the gospel. *Verdict* had been a great blessing to many people, including me, and Brinsmead had published two or three of my articles over a period of several years.

If my name created sparks within a certain fringe element of my own denomination, the name of Robert D. Brinsmead set off a fireworks show worthy of July Fourth among Seventh-day Adventists. Originally an Adventist himself, he was for decades a reformer or a rebel, depending on one's point of view, finally leaving the denomination entirely.

In the process of separating from the church, Brinsmead told me, he had gradually abandoned all the distinctive Adventist doctrines except one—the belief that hell will be a place of total, everlasting destruction rather than unending conscious torment, as most Christians believe. Now he had decided to study that subject afresh and decide whether he should reject it as unscriptural or continue to teach it as biblical truth.

To assist him in his study, he had decided to hire a non-Adventist trained in theological research, who would spend a year in the Bible, the

Jewish writings from between the Testaments, and in church history, then provide Brinsmead all the materials with any notes.

Brinsmead had seen an article of mine in *Christianity Today* titled "Putting Hell in Its Place," published in August 1976. The piece was mildly provocative, although at that time I held the traditional view on the subject. Apparently concluding that I was both competent and objective for the task, Brinsmead came to my home in Alabama to discuss the project and hopefully to return home with my commitment.

He offered a modest but respectful stipend and reimbursement of all expenses. I accepted the assignment and, in ways I could not then have believed or even imagined, changed the course of my life and my legacy. No sponsor could have been more helpful, attentive, or unselfish. He located resources that I identified but was unable to find. He faithfully and promptly reimbursed every conceivable expense—especially appreciated because cash flow, even with the print shop job, continued to be tight.

13 A RESEARCH PROJECT BEGINS

For the next year, I devoted approximately forty hours each week to the research project, in addition to my regular forty-hour job as type-setter. Being myself obsessive-compulsive in temperament, the project quickly became the priority as well, to the neglect of my family. I later confessed that to my wife and asked her forgiveness.

Each Friday when I got off work at the printing company, Sara Faye would have packed our family of four for an overnight trip to her parents in Franklin, Tennessee, about eighty miles north of our home in Athens, Alabama. She and the children, Melanie (age 5-6) and Jeremy (age 3-4) would stay there. I would drive twenty more miles into Nashville to the Vanderbilt Divinity Library, do research until the library closed, and join the family for the night.

When the library opened on Saturday morning, I was there waiting. I worked until Saturday evening, copying hundreds of pages of new mate-rials, which I carried home to pore over the following week.

I had been taught unending torment all my life. Nobody suggested that the subject of hell might be complicated, and I honestly expected to learn nothing more than a few details. But, like most Christians, I had never read one presentation of the biblical grounds supposedly support-ing the traditional view. After prayerful reflection, I decided to begin my study by reading books written in defense of the traditional view, followed by books against that view. From all these readings I listed scripture citations, as starters for my own direct Bible study.

There were considerably fewer books then on the subject of final punishment than now, and library cards reflected almost no interest in any of them, on any side of the subject. As I read the books promoting and defending everlasting torment, I became aware of a sort of unstated pattern to the argument.

Every author I found who promoted and defended the traditionalist view—the view traditionally taught by most Christians, which sees hell as a place of everlasting conscious torment—generally believed four fundamental pillars to be true.

Some authors explicitly argued one or more specific pillars as a basis for a conclusion. Other authors simply asserted the pillars without argument. Others merely assumed them and took them for granted. But regardless of the differences in presentation, these four pillars formed the foundation beneath the traditionalist's case.

(1) The Old Testament says nothing about hell.

(2) Between the time of the Old and New Testaments, the doctrine of unending conscious torment developed from Old Testament principles. By the time of Jesus, it had become "the Jewish view" in Palestine. When we read Jesus' teaching, we should assume that he held the same view and interpret what he says accordingly.

(3) New Testament writers follow Jesus and teach unending conscious torment.

(4) The immortality of the soul requires unending conscious torment unless those in hell are restored to God and join him in heaven.

As I read these arguments in defense of unending conscious torment again and again, the seriousness of what I was seeing became very clear. Either these pillars are true or they are not. They are declaratory statements of fact, and they can be verified or disproved. For the next few months, it would be my challenge to identify, collect, and summarize evidence in a way that would enable a thoughtful person to determine which verdict is appropriate.

I did not know it then, but for at least sixteen centuries, since the time of St. Augustine, the overwhelming majority of the church has accepted unending conscious torment without question. Could all those people be mistaken? What if the pillars of traditionalism's hell crumbled upon investigation?

As I began this first phase of my project, I could not possibly know, and had no reason even to suspect, the number or the nature of the surprises awaiting me on the trail I was about to explore. Those are the surprises I found in the Bible, and they are the surprises I will share with you in the rest of this book.

Everlasting Torment: Pillar 1

OLD TESTAMENT SAYS NOTHING ABOUT HELL
According to the traditional view of everlasting torment, the Old Testament does not say anything about hell. Therefore, it is implied, we need not spend time reading the Old Testament in hopes of learning anything on this subject.

---

14 SURPRISING PICTURES OF DIVINE JUSTICE

If we ask what the Old Testament says about *hell*, meaning a place where people are kept alive to be tormented forever, the answer will be "nothing." That picture is not in the Old Testament. If we look in the Greek Old Testament for *gehenna*, the word translated "hell" in the New Testament, again we will find nothing. But if we go to the Old Testament asking what it says about *the end of the wicked*, we will meet our first great surprise. And we will learn very much indeed, from all parts of the Old Testament, through at least three methods of teaching.

For example, the Psalms contain much teaching based on principles of divine justice. This is teaching designed to answer the question that recurs in every generation, in a world where righteous people sometimes suffer and wicked persons sometimes die full and happy.

The Psalms especially are filled with reminders of divine justice. Psalm 37 provides one of many such texts. This psalm begins by urging the reader not to be envious of the wicked man, even though he prospers now (v. 1). His end will be to wither and fade away like grass that dies (v. 2). He will be cut off and perish. He will vanish and be no more, the psalm assures (v. 9-10, 20). In fact, it says, wait for the Lord to act, because you will see this happen (v. 34).

But what if we do not see it now? Is God's justice thwarted? Sometimes the wicked person dies rich, happy, and honored by his community. When that happens has God been displaced as judge? Are God's principles of divine justice annulled? When we do not see justice done now, is that the last word?

That is not the end, as we know. God is still on the throne, and the wicked person will certainly answer to God—whether now or later. Even death does not let the wicked escape unjudged. God's absolute justice is not meted out here and now, but a day of divine justice is coming.

The Psalms use more than fifty verbs to assure us of the certainty of God's justice. They declare, for example, that the wicked will:

> wither (Psalm 37:2),
> be no more (Psalm 104:35),
> perish (Psalm 1:6),
> vanish (Psalm 37:20), and
> be destroyed (Psalm 37:38).

We know this will happen because God is the one who will do it. In other passages throughout the Psalms, God says that he will tend to the wicked people himself, and that he will:

> break them in pieces (Psalm 2:9),
> slay them (Psalm 139:19),
> cut them off (Psalm 94:23),
> blot them out of the book of the living (Psalm 69:28), and
> rain fire & brimstone (Psalm 11:6).

The Psalms employ at least seventy similes to tell us that when these things happen the wicked will be like:

> chaff blown away (Psalm 1:4),

a snail that melts (Psalm 58:8),
grass cut down (Psalm 37:2),
wax that melts (Psalm 68:2),
a clay pot broken (Psalm 2:9),
water that flows away (Psalm 58:7),
smoke that vanishes (Psalm 68:2), and
stubble before the wind (Psalm 83:13).

To be sure, these are not literal descriptions. The wicked will not become oversize snails, or turn into straw or wax, or be changed like magic into clay pots. But even though these statements are not literal, they are accurate. The reality will correspond to the picture stated. When people see God's justice carried out, the picture God has stated in his principles will not be the exact opposite of the thing that finally happens.

Finally, this variety of pictures, similes, and metaphors create a general impression in our minds. What is the general impression in your mind at this point? Do the images these word pictures conjure up appear to be more consistent with a fire that *torments forever,* a fire that *purifies,* or a fire that *consumes?*

15 TWO SURPRISING PREVIEWS

As we read the books of Moses, we encounter two surprising previews of the end that awaits those who reject God and his grace throughout this life. These previews come in the form of two great historical prototypes, examples in advance of what will befall the wicked at the end. They are the Flood and the destruction of Sodom and Gomorrah.

The Flood

We are all familiar with the story of the Flood, an act of divine judgment against a wicked world that once was. The picture is clear. There is no mistaking what took place. No one is confused by the language. We do not wonder if the words that tell the effects of this divine judgment are literal or figurative. We hear the story and immediately visualize it without difficulty or effort.

Genesis 7:21-23 sums up the result of the Flood like this: "Every living being on the face of the earth *perished . . . died . . .* God *blotted out* them all." We know what these words describe. We do not wonder at their meanings. In this context of judgment, we never consider reading these words figuratively. Their meanings are crystal clear to all.

When we turn to the New Testament, to our surprise we hear Peter say that this Flood we just reviewed is a sample of what awaits the wicked at the end of the world. In his second epistle, Peter writes: "For . . . the heavens existed long ago and the earth was formed out of water ... through which the world at that time was destroyed, being flooded with water. But ... the present heavens and earth are being reserved for fire , kept for the day of judgment and destruction of ungodly men" (2 Peter 3:5-7).

According to Peter, the old world was destroyed by water in the past, and the present world will be destroyed by fire in the future. Peter states one similarity: both worlds are *destroyed.* We know what that means in the first unit of the first pair. There is every reason to assume the same meaning of *destroy* in the case of the second unit as well. Peter also affirms one difference: the first world was destroyed by *water;* the second will be by *fire.* The same fire will also *destroy* "ungodly men."

Sodom's destruction

The second prototype of divine judgment from the Books of Moses is God's destruction of Sodom and Gomorrah. Again we know what happened and what that meant. God rained fire and brimstone from heaven and everything in Sodom was wiped out. Again Peter surprises us by saying that when God "condemned the cities of Sodom and Gomorrah to *destruction* by *reducing* them *to ashes,"* he "made them an *example* to those who would live ungodly lives thereafter" (2 Peter 2:6).

Jude adds to Peter's surprise with one of his own. He reaffirms that Sodom and Gomorrah "are *exhibited* as an *example* in undergoing the punishment of *eternal fire"* (Jude 7). If we did not have the Bible's own definition of "eternal fire," we might assume that it was fire that burned forever and never went out.

However, we have Jude's own statement that Sodom and Gomorrah are *examples* of "eternal fire." Sodom's fire is not still burning, but what it burned will never be seen in this world again. That is what makes "eternal" fire *eternal*—the fact that its *destruction* is *permanent* and that it will never be reversed.

16 PROPHETIC SURPRISES: Broken pottery & battlefield victims

The Jewish Bible that we call our Old Testament also contains many straightforward predictions of God's judgment awaiting the wicked at the end of the world. When we read them and visualize what we are reading, we realize that God has wrapped more surprises in packages of direct prophecies.

We do not wish to take any passage out of context or to impose a meaning on it which a Scripture writer did not intend and would not approve. The texts that follow all include specific predictions of God's future judgment. We can know that each text is talking about that subject, either by its Old Testament context or because a New Testament author ties the text to Jesus the Messiah who will carry out God's end-time judgment. Finally, let me add that these are only a few of many such texts. I also want to assure you that the picture they portray is consistent with the image found in those other texts.

Broken pottery

The wicked will be like smashed pottery (Psalm 2:7-9). This is a clear messianic Psalm as interpreted by New Testament writers, and it contains three scenes. First, we see the rebellious nations plotting against God and his Messiah. Second, Messiah speaks (the part we notice here). Third, the narrator warns the nations to submit while they can receive a blessing or face God's judgment through his Messiah. This is the central portion that includes Messiah's words.

"I will proclaim the LORD's decree: He said to me, 'You are my son; today I have begotten you. Ask me, and I will make the nations your inheritance, the ends of the earth your possession. You will *break them* with a rod of iron; you will *dash them to pieces* like *pottery*'" (Psalm 2:7-9).

We all have seen dishes made of clay—pottery, we call it. These bowls and plates and cups are plentiful around the world and nowhere more than in the Middle East. There the working poor use clay dishes most of the time. So plentiful are these pottery pieces that they are sometimes disposable: instead of washing a clay pot to use it again, one might simply use it and then throw it aside into a pile of other used, discarded, broken pots.

The key word here is *broken.* A shattered pot is thoroughly broken. One would scarcely find a more vivid example of literal brokenness than a piece of shattered pottery. That is the picture Psalm 2 gives us of the final end of the wicked.

Battlefield victims

The wicked will be like corpses on a battlefield (Psalm 110:5-6). The first verse of this Psalm is the most-mentioned Old Testament verse in the New Testament. It is quoted or cited more than twenty times, in Matthew, Mark, Luke, Acts, Romans, 1 Corinthians, Ephesians, Colossians, Hebrews, 1 Peter, and Revelation (at least). Verse four of this Psalm is a theme verse for the author of Hebrews, who discusses every phrase of the verse somewhere in the book of Hebrews.

Verses 5-6 of Psalm 110 provide our next picture of the final destiny of the wicked when Messiah judges at the end of the world. The Psalmist describes the judgment like this: "The Lord is at your right hand; he will *crush kings* on the day of his wrath. He will judge the nations, *heaping up the dead,* and *crushing the rulers* of the whole earth" (Psalm 110:5-6).

This second prophetic prediction shows us a picture of dead men, of bodies being thrown into stacks. Piles of corpses. This is the way we can imagine the end of sinners, says Psalm 110. After you visualize pottery dishes being smashed to pieces, think of a pile of enemy corpses on a battlefield. It's a scene as old as human war. It is also a significant scene, with a meaning that is instantly understandable by people around the world.

17 PROPHETIC SURPRISES:
Unburied dead bodies

Our next image of the end shows the wicked as unburied corpses tossed into an open city dump (Isaiah 66:24). If Bible passages won Oscars, this scene from the end of Isaiah could easily sweep the prizes almost any year you might choose. It would capture the medal for "most familiar" picture and also "most frequently mentioned," but surprisingly it would also win "most ignored" and "most misrepresented."

How can all these things be true at the same time? Because this is where so many people get tripped up, let's spend a moment just making sure we understand what this image of final punishment actually includes and does not include.

Isaiah 66, the chapter at the end of Isaiah, begins with God coming in vengeance against his enemies who refused his offered peace. The narrator says "those slaughtered by the Lord shall be many." Make no mistake about it—God's side finally wins! Every time. No exceptions.

There are plenty of moments during the "game" when things appear differently on earth. Especially if you are Moses on one of those many occasions when the stubborn, rebellious Israelites are complaining that they would prefer to die as slaves in Egypt of some known cause than to perish in the wilderness from some unknown hazard they cannot even name.

It doesn't always look like God's side will win in the Old Testament. Such as when the Babylonians are lowering Shadrach, Meshach, and Abednego into the fiery furnace for refusing to worship the king's image. Or when the Persians drop Daniel in the lion's den for praying to the true God and not to the king. Of course, those stories have happy endings even in this life, but some other stories do not.

The writer of Hebrews 11 mentions some of those other stories. Isaiah's story, the prophet cut in two with a wooden saw. The godly Maccabean mother—watching her seven sons tortured to death one by one, encouraging them all the while to remain firm in their allegiance to God.

The New Testament adds its own tales of heroism and great faith. John the Baptist is beheaded by a drunk and lecherous king. James is murdered with a sword. Jesus himself is crucified. John is exiled to Patmos, where he sees visions of Christ's martyrs calling "How long, O Lord, how long?"

The imagery we look at now in the closing verse of Isaiah 66 is very important in light of all these stories. This scene reassures us that God will have the last word. The final victory belongs to the faithful. Jesus was right when he urged his disciples not to fear man who could kill the body, but instead to fear God who can destroy both soul and body in hell. And what are the details that make this scene so encouraging? Let's notice them one by one.

Isaiah 66:24 is the last photograph except one in the prophet's album. Isaiah has shown God slaughtering the rebellious. He has pictured the righteous at peace in the New Jerusalem, blessed and happy forever. Now he adds a final scene of God's everlasting victory over all evil. Speaking of the redeemed, the prophet writes: "Then they will go forth and look on the corpses of the men who have transgressed against Me. For their worm will not die, and their fire will not be quenched, and they will be an abhorrence to all mankind" (Isaiah 66:24).

In this final picture of the wicked, Isaiah underscores the final and everlasting defeat of God's enemies with four powerful images. They are dead. They are unburied. They are disappearing. They are disgusting.

Isaiah identifies the wicked as "the corpses" of God's adversaries. Corpses are powerless. They cannot harm anyone. Regardless of their advantageous position over the righteous while alive, *corpses* enjoy no such advantages. This final picture of the wicked is a picture of corpses.

These corpses are unburied. It would be disgraceful to drag the body of a dead person into the front yard and leave it there exposed. It would be even worse to haul a corpse to the old-fashioned city dump and toss it there—a place of smoldering piles of garbage, of dead and rotting animals, a place of consuming fires and devouring maggots.

But that is the picture before us now. Further, these corpses are disappearing, because the fires and the worms are doing the very thing they are supposed to do—consuming the corpses. These agents of destruction are relentless. They do not stop consuming.

The fire will burn and the maggots will devour so long as anything is left to devour. Nothing stops them from their task. The fire is not extinguished. The worm does not die. Some day nothing will be left of these corpses. Then the fires can go out and the worms can finally die. But not a moment before.

This is a picture of *dead corpses,* not living people. They are being *destroyed,* not tormented. The worms and fire *consume,* they do not torture. People who see this scene find it *repulsive,* not sad. The observers feel *disgust* and not pity. This is a picture of the way it will be with the wicked at the end of the world.

Jesus was not yet born when someone began to change the picture— essentially reversing all its details—making it exactly opposite to the picture that Isaiah had given. We will return to discuss these when we come to the Apocrypha.

18 PROPHETIC SURPRISES: Total burnup

The Old Testament closes with one of its most graphic descriptions of the end of the wicked. It is also one of the most unmistakable images, leaving no room for doubt concerning the total destruction it portrays. The prophet says: "The day is coming, burning like a furnace; and . . . every evildoer will be chaff; and the day . . . will set them ablaze," says the LORD of hosts, "so that it will leave them neither root nor branch." The wicked "will be ashes under the soles of your feet on the day which I am preparing," says the LORD of hosts (Malachi 4:1-3).

The scene progresses step by step in predictable order. Evildoers are like chaff, the highly-flammable, almost-explosive outer shell of the wheat. The day of God's judgment ignites them. They are totally burned up—nothing is left, neither root at one end nor branch at the other. Nothing but ashes remains to remind that the wicked ever existed.

These pictures are not necessarily literal. Even so, those who see the fulfillment will remember the prophecy and will say that the two things match. The reality will not be the exact opposite of its description that is given to us now.

Advocates of everlasting torment read the Old Testament, do not find their view in it, and conclude that it has nothing to say on the subject of final punishment. Instead of seeking some specific picture of hell, I went to the Old Testament asking if it had anything to say about the end of the wicked. To my great surprise, it answered with principles, proto-types, and prophecies. In each case, the material left a general impression. Sometimes the Old Testament author left specific prophetic detail as well.

Now that we have considered what the Old Testament says about the end of the wicked, ask yourself again: What general *impression* do you get from the Old Testament on this topic? Do these prototypes and predictions sound more like a fire that *torments forever,* a fire that *purifies,* or a fire that *consumes?*

Does your answer surprise you as much as my answer surprised me?

Everlasting Torment: Pillar 2

ONE 'JEWISH VIEW' IN THE TIME OF JESUS

Pillar Two of the traditional view states that the doctrine of everlasting torment developed during the four hundred years between Malachi and Matthew. By the time Jesus was born, everlasting conscious torment had become "the Jewish view" held by everyone Jesus encountered. We should therefore assume that Jesus also held this view, according to this pillar, and interpret all his teachings based on that assumption.

19   FOUR CENTURIES

Between the days of Malachi at the end of the Old Testament era and the announcement and birth of John the Baptist at the beginning of the New Testament Gospels is a period of about four hundred years. Four centuries. A block of history equal to the period from the settlement of the Jamestown Colony in the New World colony of Virginia and the publication of the King James Version of the Bible until today. Now that's a long time. But that is how much time went by between our Old and New Testament Scriptures.

Naturally the generations of people who lived during the four intertestamental centuries did not consider themselves or their place in history to be irrelevant. They worked, played, had families, and taught and thought—and wrote some of what they thought for posterity, some of which we still have.

The Jewish literature during this time is sometimes called the intertestamental literature, meaning that it arose during the time between the Old and New Testaments. It is sometimes called the literature of Second Temple Judaism, because these centuries included the time when King Herod the Great rebuilt the Jerusalem Temple that had been destroyed by Nebuchadnezzar of Babylon years before. Herod's Temple stood until it was destroyed by the Roman armies in A.D. 69-70.

This Jewish literature between Malachi and Matthew can be divided into three major groupings known as the *Apocrypha,* the *Pseudepigrapha,* and the *Dead Sea Scrolls*. The authors of these three groups of literature held a variety of views about the final end of the wicked. In fact, the same three views that have been held by Christians throughout church history are also found within the Jewish literature from the years between the Testaments.

20 THE APOCRYPHA

The *Apocrypha* is best known today as the collection of Old Testament books found in the Catholic Bible but not in the Protestant Bible. A hundred years and more after Malachi, Alexander the Great conquered the Mediterranean world. One important effect was the spread of Greek language and culture wherever "civilized" people were found.

During this period, Jewish scholars at Alexandria in Egypt translated the Hebrew Bible of the Jews into the spoken Greek of the common people. This translation, which tradition says had seventy translators, is called the Septuagint, the Greek word for "seventy," and is abbreviated as the LXX (Roman numeral for 70). The *Apocrypha* are the books that were included in the Septuagint, but were never a part of the Hebrew Bible.

On the subject of final punishment, the Apocrypha agrees with the Old Testament, with one notable exception in the Book of Judith, which tells the story of a Jewish heroine who saves the Jews from the murderous plots of pagan king Holofernes. The final verse of Judith contains a warning against any others who might entertain similar evil designs.

Judith wrote: "Woe to the nations that rise up against my race; the Lord Almighty will take vengeance against them in the day of judgment, to put fire and worms in their flesh; and they will weep and feel their pain forever" (Judith 16:17).

It is clear that Judith 16:17 is based on the picture we saw already in Isaiah 66:24—a picture of a city dump with smoldering fires and hungry maggots, competing with each other to consume dead corpses of God's enemies that had been discarded there as garbage. But it is also clear that Judith changes Isaiah's picture . . . so drastically that we can safely say she completely reverses the point the prophet made in his book.

Isaiah pictures *dead corpses;* Judith talks about living people. Isaiah's corpses are *consumed* by external fire and maggot; Judith's people are tormented by internal fire and worm. Isaiah's scene suggests *shame* and evokes our *disgust;* Judith's scene suggests pain and evokes our pity. In short, Isaiah paints a word-picture totally consistent with the teaching of the whole Old Testament, and (as we will shortly see) of the New Testament as well. It is a scene of total and irreversible extinction.

Judith changes Isaiah's picture of the fire that *consumes* into a clear picture of the fire that *torments forever.* This is the first time we see this fire that *torments*—in anything related to Jewish scriptural literature. Unfortunately, it will not be the last.

21 RABBIS, SCROLLS, AND NOT-REALLYS

During these years, rabbis were passing down the oral explanations of the Torah (Books of Moses) to a younger generation of rabbis. This oral tradition was eventually written down as the Mishna and, later, the Talmud. These rulings and reasonings of the rabbis are summarized by German scholars Strack and Billerbeck.

Rabbinic materials

The dates covered are uncertain, but according to Strack and Billerbeck, the rabbis during the century or two after Jesus Christ were divided in opinion about hell or *gehenna*. Some expected a fire that *torments* either temporarily or even *forever*, others a fire that *purifies*, and others a fire that *consumes*. That certainly comes as a surprise to anyone who thought that all Jews of Jesus' day expected the wicked to burn alive forever in hell.

But Strack and Billerbeck have another surprise as well. According to these scholars, when the authors of the Jewish literature between the Testaments spoke of everlasting torment in hell, they might have used even that language to symbolize total and irreversible annihilation.

Dead Sea Scrolls

Perhaps the best known Jewish writings of the period between the Testaments are the Dead Sea Scrolls, thought to have been written and finally hidden by a community of sectarian Jews. These Jews, seeking a purer religious life, had separated themselves from the corrupt religious establishment at Jerusalem to follow the ways of the Lord in the desert at Qumran near the Dead Sea.

Some scrolls describe a final world battle between forces of good and evil. Others detail the rules of life in the Qumran community. Many are commentaries on biblical (our Old Testament) books—which "accidentally" provided modern scholars with Hebrew biblical texts one thousand years older than the oldest texts they had ever seen.

More than eight hundred scrolls and fragments of scrolls now have been found and translated into English. It appears that the community that produced the Scrolls at Qumran consistently expected the wicked finally to be destroyed and gone forever. It is not always clear whether the authors of the Scrolls expected the wicked to perish in the final war between good and evil, to survive that battle (or to be raised after dying in it) and then be destroyed by God, or perhaps to become extinct through some combination of those events.

What does seem clear, however, is that the Dead Sea Scrolls look for a fire that *consumes.* They do not mention anything that resembles a fire that *torments forever.*

Pseudepigrapha

Not included in anyone's Bible is another body of intertestamental literature called the Pseudepigrapha. The name means "false writings." It is given because these books claimed to have been written by ancient Jews and their ancestors—Adam and Eve, Enoch, Moses, and other people who lived and died long before the books appeared bearing their names.

If we imagine modern literary critics living in those days, we can almost see a critic refer to the Pseudepigrapha authors as "the not-reallys."

The Pseudepigrapha offer mixed views about the end of the wicked. Some books expect a fire that *consumes* until the wicked no longer exist anywhere. A book known as Psalms of Solomon speaks of a day when sinners "will be taken away into destruction, and their memorial will be found no more" (Ps. Sol. 13:11).

Other books look for a fire that *torments*, sometimes for a limited period of time, sometimes apparently forever. One such book speaks of a place that is "everywhere fire, and everywhere frost and ice, thirst and shivering, while the bonds are very cruel, and the angels fearful and merciless, bearing angry weapons, merciless torture" (2 Enoch 10:1-6).

Summary

The important truth from all this is that when Jesus was teaching, there was no such thing as "the Jewish view" on hell, but rather there was a variety of opinion on this subject. We therefore cannot assume that Jesus held a particular view based on any supposed unanimity of Jewish opinion. Instead we investigate each teaching of Jesus with open mind and open heart to discover its meaning. When we do that, we discover that Jesus' teaching on final punishment, as on other subjects, was rooted in Old Testament revelation, which it sometimes advanced but never contradicted.

22 WHAT DID JESUS ACTUALLY SAY?

We come now to the New Testament, where the first word of teaching about the end of the wicked comes from John the Baptist. Malachi, the last Old Testament writing prophet, had predicted John's coming four hundred years before his birth. Interestingly, when John appears, his first words about final punishment portray the same picture with which Malachi had closed his book.

John's primary task and message was to introduce Jesus as the Lamb of God, the Savior of the world. But this happy announcement carried with it a call to repentance and a warning of judgment. John pictured Jesus as the harvester at the end of the world.

"I baptize you with water for repentance," said John. "but he who is coming after me is mightier than I . . . . His winnowing fork is in his hand, and he will thoroughly clear his threshing floor; and he will gather his wheat into the barn, but he will *burn up* the chaff with *unquenchable fire*" (Matt. 3:11-12).

Malachi had closed the Old Testament by predicting a day when the wicked would be set ablaze, the fire would leave them neither root nor branch, and they would become ashes under the soles of the feet of the righteous. Now John pictures the same end for the wicked at the hands of Jesus, who will *burn up* the chaff (wicked people). Because this fire cannot be resisted or extinguished, it will continue to burn until it has thoroughly burned up whatever is put into it.

It is often said that Jesus speaks more about hell than anyone else in the Bible. That is true, if one means that Jesus uses the Greek word for hell (*gehenna*) more than any other person. If we do not require that particular word, the prize for "most said" goes to Paul instead.

Now it is time for us to look more closely at this special word and see what surprises it also might hold for our inquiry.

The word *gehenna* was formed from the phrase "valley (of the sons) of Hinnom," a literal place south of the city of Jerusalem. In ancient times, this valley was a site of idol worship involving the burning of infants. It was an abominable place in God's sight, and he prophesied that in the future it would be desecrated and despised. This valley is most likely the historic site in Isaiah's picture of future punishment, described in Isaiah 66:24, where exposed corpses are consumed by fire and maggots.

For many centuries it has been said that this valley was the open garbage dump for Jerusalem in the time of Jesus. That is now widely questioned, and it cannot be proven, although there is some archaeological evidence that supports the idea. Whether the literal valley of Hinnom was a garbage dump then or not really makes no difference.

The scene described in Isaiah 66:24 clearly has all the same connotations as an open city dump. Further, the name *gehenna* began to be used during the intertestamental period for the place of final punishment. Jesus himself quotes Isaiah 66:24 and applies its language to *gehenna* as the place of final punishment in Mark 9.

Most important to us is what Jesus says about *gehenna* and what happens there. Is its fire one that torments forever? Or does it purify? Or is it a fire that consumes? Here's one answer from the Lord himself. "Do not fear those who kill the body but are unable to kill the soul," the Savior admonishes, "but rather fear Him who is able to *destroy* both soul and body in hell" (Matt. 10:28).

It seems straightforward enough, doesn't it? Both God and man can be intimidating. But we need not fear man, Jesus explains, for his reach is limited by comparison with God's. Men can kill the body but they cannot kill the soul. God, on the other hand, is able to destroy both soul and body in hell.

And in case someone is tempted to give "destroy" some novel meaning in that sentence, Jesus makes it plain that he is using "destroy" here to mean what "kill" meant in the earlier part of the sentence. And "kill" means the same thing here when used of body or of soul.

If any different shade of meaning is intended, the way Jesus uses the words "kill" and "destroy" here strongly suggests that "destroy" is the weightier word of the two. "Destroy" clearly is intended to include all that the previous clause meant to include in "kill." While it might mean more than "kill" in the usual sense of that word, it certainly means no less!

23 WHY CAN'T WORDS MEAN WHAT THEY SAY?

To someone of a different opinion, the folks who argue for unending conscious torment seem to have a strange habit with the meanings of words. Here's the complaint. When the biblical authors talk about final punishment, they use some words and phrases so often and so regularly that those words and phrases can rightly be called "key words." But whenever the good people who argue for the majority view talk about biblical texts that contain those key words, they find it impossible to let these words mean what they most naturally seem to say.

For example, the word translated "destroy" in Matthew 10:28 is the same Greek word that is translated "perish" in John 3:16. And, along with the words "die" and "death," these two words "perish" and "destroy" are the words New Testament writers use most often to tell what will finally happen to the unredeemed.

But when the advocates of the traditional hell read John 3:16 and hear Jesus say that believers (in contrast to rejecters) will not *perish* but have eternal *life*, or when they read Jesus' warning in Matthew 10:28 to fear God who is able to *destroy* both soul and body in hell, they automatically go into their define-with-opposite-meanings mode.

"Perish" does not mean "perish" here, they say; "destroy" surely cannot mean "destroy." In fact, when these words are used to describe what will become of the wicked in hell, they mean that the wicked will *never* "perish" as that word is commonly used, and they will *never* be "destroyed" in the ordinary sense of that word.

So instead of letting simple words have their usual simple meanings (which is the simplest way of doing things), the scholars who teach everlasting torment go looking for other texts of Scripture that use "perish" and "destroy" in a figurative sense. Two such passages are Matthew 9:17, which speaks of "ruined" wineskins (using the same Greek word translated "perish" and "destroy"), and John 6:12, that talks about "spoiled" food (for the same Greek adjective translated "perish" and "destroy").

Jesus does not mean that God will really "destroy" the soul, the unending-torment defenders argue. He does not mean that rejecters really "perish." What Jesus is trying to tell us, they explain, is that people who are not saved will be "ruined" (like old wineskins). They will "spoil" like bad food. And what those words are trying to communicate, the defenders of the traditional view explain, is that those who finally go to hell will actually be kept alive forever for the single purpose of being tormented without end.

But does that explanation really make sense? If *that* is what Jesus is thinking, he needs only to say that believers "will not live forever in torment but have eternal life." And wouldn't it have been much simpler to have said "fear God who is able *never* to kill soul and body but instead to keep them alive and torment them forever"—IF that is really what he wanted us to understand?

24 SURPRISE:
Perish and destroy
can mean just that

But isn't it possible that words like "perish" and "destroy" sometimes have figurative meanings, and that we should think of those meanings when the Bible says that the unredeemed finally perish and are destroyed? It goes without saying that "perish" and "destroy," like most other words, can be used in a figurative sense. Of course the New Testament sometimes uses the word translated "perish" and "destroy" in a secondary sense with a non-literal meaning. But we should also remember that the only reason words can have secondary meanings is because they have primary meanings first.

To say it another way, if we say that someone *perishes*, we usually mean that they *die* or that they are *destroyed*. That is the primary, literal meaning of the word *perish*. If we want to say that food goes bad, we can say that, or we can use *perish* in a secondary or figurative sense and say the food *perished*. But the only reason *perish* has a secondary meaning is because it had a primary meaning first.

Because almost every advocate of eternal torment makes this "figurative meaning" argument about *perish* and *destroy* every time the Bible says the wicked will finally *perish* and be *destroyed,* someone might go away thinking that the words *perish* and *destroy* usually mean something other than their simple meaning as we all understand it.

That is not the reality, however. And because it is so very much not the reality, it might be helpful if we take a moment to notice how New Testament writers use *perish* and *destroy* most often. Or, in other words, we need to be sure we understand the common, usual, regular, ordinary, literal, primary meaning of those two words (and of the Greek word behind them both in the New Testament).

So here goes! Whatever word any particular translation or version of the New Testament might use, the original Greek verb in each of these passages is the same word translated *perish* in John 3:16, and *destroy* in Matthew 10:28. As you read each sentence, ask yourself the original, ordinary, plain meaning of each main verb.

1. The disciples are about to *perish* in a storm (Matt 8:25).
2. The Pharisees seek to *destroy* Jesus (Matt 12:14).
3. Someone *loses their life* trying to save it (Matt 16:25).
4. A vineyard owner *executes* the murderous tenants (Matt 21:41).
5. A king sends his troops to *destroy* murderers (Matt 22:7).
6. Someone *perishes* by the sword (Matt 26:52).
7. The crowd asks to *destroy* Jesus (Matt 27:20).
8. The high priest says it is better that one man die, than for a whole nation to *perish* (John 11:50).
9. An insurrectionist/false messiah *perished* at the hands of Rome (Acts 5:37).
10. Many Israelites *perished* in the wilderness (1 Cor. 10:9-10), or were *destroyed* there (Jude 5).
11. Some people *perished* in the rebellion of Korah (Jude 11).

It's quite obvious that the authors of these eleven sentences expect us to read these verbs of destruction with their basic, face-value meaning, isn't it? Why should we not understand "perish" and "destroy" equally literally in John 3:16 and in Matthew 10:28?

25 SURPRISE:
Teeth gnashing means anger, not pain

But what about all those expressions Jesus uses to describe people who go to hell? For example, who has not heard of the gnashing (grinding) of teeth? And can't you just picture the scene? There's the poor guy in hell, in terrible agony, suffering in silence, grinding his teeth in pain that never goes away.

Well, yes, I can visualize that if I try, but why try to imagine a scene that has absolutely no support anywhere in the Bible? Before you write me off as hopelessly ignorant, let me quickly explain. The expression "weeping and gnashing of teeth" certainly comes from the Bible . . . to be more specific, from the Gospels . . . indeed (as with the word *gehenna*) from the lips of the Lord Jesus Christ himself and from him alone. There is no dispute about that.

But if we presently think that teeth-gnashing in Jesus' comments indicates pain, *and* if we will allow the Bible to explain its own symbols, we are about to discover another surprise. Two surprises, in fact. First, that when Jesus mentions gnashing of teeth, pain is *not* the point. Second, that when the Bible speaks of someone gnashing teeth, it means that person is very, very *angry.*

When I was growing up in the Deep South long ago, a preacher supposedly was explaining the gnashing of teeth when one of his listeners called out, "What will they do when the man grinds his teeth completely away?" To which the preacher replied, "Well, the Lord does not say specifically, but I suppose he will just give the poor fellow another set of teeth."

Let us look closely at the seven stories in which Jesus describes people grinding their teeth. In each situation, the teeth-gnasher has been tossed out of a previous location. Not only that, he has been evicted into circumstances far less pleasant than the ones he recently enjoyed. One teeth-gnasher is expelled from the kingdom (Luke 13:28), another one from an unnamed place (Matt. 24:50-51).

Three times the destination is described as "outer darkness" (Matt. 8:11-12; 22:13; 25:30). To let that imagery sink in, just imagine a party at night in a brightly-lit house. Suddenly the host points to a particular guest, nods to the official "bouncer," and the burly fellow unceremoniously tosses the unwanted chap into the darkness outside, where we later hear that he is still gnashing his teeth.

Twice he is expelled *to* a furnace of fire (Matt. 13:40-42, 49-50). Do we think it curious that five of the seven teeth-gnashers are in fire-free stories? These seven situations involve nothing inherently painful—other than the two furnaces, and Jesus does not relate the teeth-gnashing there to high temperature. Someone asks about the weeping. It is a natural point of curiosity, but one with many reasonable explanations other than pain.

For one of the clearest examples of the meaning of teeth-gnashing, we turn to Acts 7:52-54, where the holy martyr Stephen is about to be rushed by a blood-thirsty mob and stoned to death. Stephen accuses them of killing Jesus, God's "righteous one." Enraged, the mobsters grind their teeth at Stephen. It is clear that they are not in pain; they are crazed with *anger.*

Similarly, Psalm 112:1-9 describes the rewards and blessings the righteous inherit. Verse 10 says the wicked see it and are vexed—*angry;* no, make that *furious.* The wicked man gnashes his teeth (not in pain but in *anger*—he is vexed, remember?)

But notice this—all that teeth-gnashing finally is for nothing! The rest of the verse contains the kicker: even as he gnashes, the wicked man vanishes away. Is that a surprise, or what? (Every time I read this verse, I get a mental image of the Wicked Witch in Oz, who likewise "vanishes away" as Dorothy, Toto, and their fellow-pilgrims watch in amazement.) A satisfying surprise, indeed!

26 SURPRISE:
Talking not the same as doing

One of the biggest surprises I have encountered during the thirty-plus years of studying this subject is the gap between *profession* and *practice* regarding the final authority of Scripture. Who can believe that a Protestant theologian, much beloved and respected by a particular segment of evangelicalism even today, would ever admit:

> I have had but one object in my professional career and as a writer, and that is to state and to vindicate the doctrines of the _____ Church. I have never advanced a new idea, and have never aimed to improve on the doctrines of our fathers. Having become satisfied that the system of doctrines taught in the symbols of the _____ Churches is taught in the Bible, I have endeavored to sustain it, and am willing to believe even where I cannot understand.[12]

It is not uncommon for a traditionalist author to praise Scripture's teaching as the written word of God, then, when Scripture seems to contradict the traditionalist view, to dismiss the argument as contrary to what most theologians have always believed.

This inconsistent behavior is not new. It has been going on for about 1,600 years since St. Augustine. Earlier writers such as the unknown author of the Didache, Justin Martyr, Ignatius, and others taught the fire that *consumes,* the view throughout Scripture. Athenagoras and Tertullian urged the fire that *torments.* Clement of Alexandria, and especially his successor Origen, favored the fire that *purifies.*

In Book 21 of his massive work, *The City of God,* Augustine endorsed Tertullian's explanation of hell as the fire that *torments forever.* With Augustine in Tertullian's corner, hell could now be placed on a shelf of subjects needing no further Bible study. Everybody knew that it was no longer an open question, but was now an issue that had been settled once for all.

A thousand years later, the Reformers Luther and Calvin would draw some clear marks in the sand to help tell who was on which side. One identifying difference between the Reformers and the Reform-Resisters concerned their attitudes toward authority. Did the decision of a church council settle a doctrinal issue forever after, or were church councils themselves subject to future testing by the teaching of Scripture? The Catholics adopted the first view; the Reformers defended the second view.

It was no surprise to me when Peter, at the time a bishop in an Eastern Orthodox Church, told me that the nature of hell's fire had been decided centuries ago and that nothing useful remained to be said. Nor was I particularly disturbed when my friend John, a Roman Catholic monk, explained to me that what happens in hell is not an open question, since a church council settled the matter long ago. Both Peter and John were responding in a manner true to their convictions, and in keeping with Eastern Orthodox and Roman Catholic beliefs about authority.

What did set me back on my heels, however, was when two of the most highly respected evangelical leaders in America called 450 theologians to a four-day meeting in 1989 to discuss, vote on, and decide what evangelicals could believe on a variety of Bible subjects including the nature of hell. After some very heated speeches, a motion to condemn all views of hell except everlasting torment was voted down, but only barely.

Some of these evangelical Protestants, who had hoped to settle the hell controversy Catholic-style by the decision of a council, were disappointed. But in time they recovered and continued their careers, taking every opportunity to declare their "high view" of Scripture. And when anyone challenged the traditional view of hell by appealing to the Bible, they simply reminded the troublemaker of "what evangelicals have always taught," and turned out the lights.

For many of us, however, studying these matters afresh is a worthy goal, and so we flip the light switch to "ON" again and continue to read our Bibles seeking new illumination.

27   ETERNAL PUNISHMENT

Pretend for a moment that your mind is totally blank on the subject of this book—say you had never read one word from the Bible about hell. But today you walk into a room you have never entered before. There, spread out before your curious eyes, is a copy of every statement Jesus ever uttered about final judgment.

Your eyes dance from one text to the next. A pair of contrasting clauses grabs your attention: "These will go away into *eternal punishment,*" you read, "but the righteous into *life eternal*" (Matt. 25:46). This is Jesus speaking—Bible study is not going to get more authoritative than that. Eternal life and eternal punishment are surely easy concepts, clearly expressed—no danger of misunderstanding these words. It's all right here in black-and-white, and from the mouth of Jesus Christ himself.

The words are the punch-line of one of Jesus' most famous teachings about final judgment—the Parable of the Sheep and Goats. At the end of the age, Jesus appears and judges the nations. The issue is whether folks helped or ignored others who were in need—"the least of these, my brothers and sisters," Jesus calls them.

Jesus separates the nations into two groups, then pronounces their final fates: for the sheep, eternal life; for the goats, eternal punishment. The first thing that jumps out at us in both cases is that adjective *eternal.*

"Eternal." It is right there . . . up front . . . on both sides of the equation. Jesus says both destinies are *eternal*. But what does that tell us about either?[13] When the dust settles, this adjective *eternal* adds two special colors to the otherwise black-and-white words *life* and *punishment*.

First, the adjective colors both *life* and *punishment* as *belonging to the age to come* and not to the present age. As New Testament writers see it (taking their cue from Jesus himself), the age to come has already begun to make its appearance—when Jesus died, rose again, ascended to his seat of honor in heaven, and sent the Holy Spirit on Pentecost. But it has only begun to appear.

There are elements of God's activities, both good and bad, that will be fully known and experienced only during the fullness of the age to come. Judgment, for example, that results in redemption and salvation, on the one hand, and in punishment and destruction, on the other hand. When New Testament authors wish to speak of those elements in their connection with the age to come, they sometimes add the adjective "eternal" to indicate that perspective.

We read of eternal *salvation* (Heb. 5:9), eternal *redemption* (Heb. 9:12), eternal *judgment* (Heb. 6:2), eternal *punishment* (Matt. 25:46), and eternal *destruction* (2 Thess. 1:9). When Jesus speaks of *eternal* life and *eternal* punishment, he colors the life and the punishment "eternal," identifying them as belonging to the age to come.

The adjective "eternal" also leaves a second color on *life* and *punishment*. That is the color of *permanence*. *Eternal life* with God will never end. We will forever be with the Lord, clothed in immortality with bodies that can never die. *Eternal punishment* will also be permanent. But there is something very interesting about the permanence of the five realities mentioned in the paragraph just above this one.

Did you notice that all five of these things—salvation, redemption, judgment, punishment, and destruction—have something else in common? They all result from some action or process. Salvation is the result of *saving*. Redemption results from *redeeming*. Judgment is the result of *judging*. Punishment and destruction are results of *punishing* and *destroying*.

Now look with me one step farther. In each case above, the thing that is "eternal," the thing that the adjective "eternal" colors "permanent," is the *result* of the action, not the *action* that produces the result. Let's look at the five words one by one.

What is permanent in *eternal salvation?* The thing that continues forever is the salvation that *results,* not the process of saving that *produces* that result. In the same way, *eternal redemption* results from redeeming that stops. Eternal judgment is the result of judging *that ends.* Eternal punishment results from *punishing* that stops, and *destroying* will not continue without end, but the *destruction* that results will be everlasting.

28   ETERNAL (CAPITAL) PUNISHMENT

But we need to inquire more. What is the *punishment* that Jesus here calls *eternal?* The word "punishment" by itself tells us something about the character of the thing, but it does not give any hint or clue concerning what the thing consists of. What is "punishment?" It is simply the penal consequence of wrongdoing, imposed under the law by a person with judicial authority.

But of what does that penal consequence consist? In the United States, a state criminal code defines crimes recognized within the jurisdiction and identifies the punishment imposed by state law on anyone who commits that crime. The punishment might be a fine or time in jail. It could be one or more years of confinement in a penitentiary. It might even be life in prison. And, when the worst crimes are committed, the *punishment* for those crimes can be "capital" punishment—the death penalty—execution—forfeiture of life itself.

But none of that is in the word *punishment* standing alone. When Jesus speaks of eternal punishment, we know he is talking about penal consequences for wrongdoing. The adjective *eternal* tells us that these consequences belong to the age to come and that their result is unending. From what we have learned about *gehenna* already, we know that eternal punishment is the same as God destroying soul and body.

In 2 Thessalonians 1, Paul tells what eternal punishment will involve. When Jesus comes again, Paul writes, he will *punish* the wicked with *eternal destruction* (v. 9). Eternal punishment consists of eternal destruction. Once punished—in this case, once destroyed—the result is everlasting. The wicked will never be seen again. This is eternal capital punishment. The everlasting death penalty. The second death.

The Bible suggests that there will be different degrees of suffering by the lost, as perhaps in Jesus' statement that some will receive "few stripes" and others "many stripes" (Luke 12:47-48). We usually relate that to physical, psychological, or spiritual pains of some type or another, more or less intense, and longer or shorter in length of time endured. If those are the variables involved, the scenario we have suggested allows plenty of opportunity for that. The destructive process can accommodate any combination of elements of suffering that God might see fit to inflict— whether duration, intensity, or type of conscious pain.

The punishment suffered in hell is *capital* punishment. Or, to say it another way, eternal *punishment* is eternal *destruction*. "But wait a minute," someone objects. "If evildoers are totally destroyed, they do not suffer any pain after that. And surely it will not take very long for anyone to be destroyed. How can that possibly be called *eternal* punishment?"

"Delighted that you ask!" I respond. "And for your answer, we turn to the wisdom of St. Augustine, the very man we have credited (or blamed) for making *eternal torment* the standard orthodoxy of the Roman Catholic Church. The great church father rejected what I consider to be the biblical understanding of hell as the fire that consumes. Ironically, in reading the writings of scholars from throughout centuries of church history, I have found no one else who answers the question we are posing better than St. Augustine does.

Just to remind you, the question before us is this: "If people are totally destroyed, they no longer exist and therefore feel no pain. If hell's fire really does consume entirely and forever, how can that be called *eternal punishment?*"

Although he did not realize it at the time, St. Augustine answered that question beautifully in the following words: "Where a very serious crime is punished by death and the execution of the sentence takes only a minute, no laws consider that minute as the measure of the punishment, but rather the fact that the criminal is forever removed from the community of the living."

Ironically, if we apply St. Augustine's statement to hell, it reminds us that the punishment of the wicked consists not only of dying the second death itself and experiencing every pain suffered in the process of dying, but also the *loss* of every good blessing, every godly companion, and of every moment that might otherwise have been enjoyed in a new heavens and a new earth forever without end.

29   SURPRISE:
Eternal fire destroys forever

Although many of Jesus' teachings about the end of the wicked do not include any reference to fire at all, whoever comes to this subject still enters territory that can only be called a serious "fire zone."

That becomes obvious to any New Testament reader who pays close attention to the text, which is full of fire from beginning to end. We meet the fire of judgment at the front door. John the Baptist shouts to the "snakes" in charge of religion that the wildfire they fear cannot be extinguished to save them.

We hear Jesus' teaching that mentions the place-name *gehenna*, then we hear more from Jesus about unnamed fire that is equally ominous. And when we arrive at the back door of the New Testament, the fire is there also. Revelation, the last book of the Bible, ends with the lake of fire—which for humans, John always explains, "*is* the second death."

Surrounded by this context of fire, no one seems surprised to hear Jesus, while giving the Parable of the Sheep and Goats, mention in passing "eternal fire" (Matt. 25:41). And precisely what, we wonder, is *eternal fire?* As it happens, we have answered the question already—at least in principle—but the phrase "eternal fire" is so often misused that it seems only right to give it special attention by itself.

By calling this fire "eternal," Jesus tells us two things about it. First, this fire belongs to the age to come. We are familiar with fire already in the present age. The fire we now use, and work with, and put out when it threatens to burn something we wish to preserve, can be very destructive. A bolt of lightning at night in a deserted forest can ignite a fire that consumes thousands of acres of timber. A cigarette carelessly tossed from an automobile can start a blaze that wipes out a whole town.

Present-age fire can even kill a living person and destroy that person's physical body—as when a martyr is burned at the stake. But the fire of the present age is limited in what it can destroy. It cannot kill or destroy the soul—the person considered in her wholeness, intended for life with God in the age to come. To accomplish that result—the destruction, killing, burning up, of a whole person entirely and forever—one must have access to fire of the age to come. And, in a word, the fire of the age to come is *eternal* fire.

The word *eternal* tells us a second thing also about the judgment fire awaiting those who go to hell. In some sense, this fire has an *unending* quality about it. On this point, we are not required to guess. The Bible itself explains why the fire of the age to come is called *eternal fire* in this second sense of "eternal." That explanation is found in the tiny book of Jude, in a statement looking back to the annihilation of Sodom and Gomorrah.

We have read Jude's words before, when we discussed Sodom as a prototype of divine judgment. The comment is at verse seven in Jude's single-chapter epistle. It says that "Sodom and Gomorrah . . . are exhibited as an example, in undergoing the punishment of eternal fire."

The destruction of Sodom and Gomorrah was so sensational, so thorough, so permanent that its story alone contributed much of the language of judgment found in the rest of the Bible. The classic picture language of *fire and brimstone* comes from Sodom's story. This expression is the way older English translations speak of the burning sulfur that "rained" down, volcano-like, from the sky and turned that moment for Sodom into the end of the world.

The figure of *ascending smoke* in connection with divine judgment also comes from Sodom's story—where, like the image of a mushroom-shaped cloud today, it symbolizes a judgment completed, life now extinguished in a place only yesterday abuzz with activity. When this word-picture in the Bible is accompanied by a comment that the smoke ascends "forever," the additional word "forever" adds the meaning that the thing burned up will never be rebuilt (Isa. 34:10).

We can now add another judgment phrase to our list of phrases from Sodom and Gomorrah. Jude says in verse seven that God has made those cities an *exhibit* of his judgment against sin. More specifically, Jude says that Sodom and Gomorrah serve as an example—a model, a sample, a prototype—"in *undergoing* the punishment of *eternal fire*."

Do we want to know what "eternal fire" looks like? We need only look at God's example of Sodom and Gomorrah. We can look back at Sodom in the past and from its fate understand the meaning of the "eternal fire" that awaits the unredeemed at the end of the world.

The fire that annihilated Sodom and Gomorrah is not still burning. It burned up the cities and everything in them. Then it went out. That fire is called *eternal fire*. It is not "eternal" because it burns forever, for it does *not* burn forever. It is called "eternal" fire because it *destroys* forever. That is what Sodom's fire did. It is what the fire of hell will do. That is the Bible's own definition of the phrase "eternal fire."

30 THE RICH MAN AND LAZARUS (1)

Blame it on the King James Version if you wish. The dangling fruit was so beautiful and far too close to resist. Imagine that you are a preacher and you have been requested to present a sermon on hell—"for the young folks," the requester explains. "Not blaming you, of course, but some members of their generation have never heard an old-fashioned, true-blue, fire-and-brimstone sermon on hell."

You flip through your favorite reading Bible. The Old Testament does not mention final hell, you remember. Wherever the word "hell" creeps into the English Old Testament, it always translates *sheol*, the Hebrew word for the unseen realm of the dead. It has nothing to do with punishment in the Old Testament—good and bad people all finally land there. The Old Testament never mentions hell as the place where the ungodly will suffer eternal punishment.[14]

The New Testament presents its own set of problems. Your concordance of Greek words reminds you that *gehenna*, the word for "hell" as final punishment, appears only twelve times in the whole New Testament. One of those is in James, where it is not talking about final punishment at all. The other eleven usages are all in the Gospels. All are spoken by Jesus to Jews who live in or around Jerusalem. As odd as it seems to us, if the New Testament reflects a typical picture of the word's usage, most of the early church might never have heard the word for "hell" at all.

Then it happens! As you skim through the Gospel of Luke, your eyes strike a word here, a phrase there. Soon you are too entangled to go anywhere else. It is the parable of the Rich Man and Lazarus. The beggar Lazarus is laid at the gate of the rich man, who ignores him—while he himself banquets daily. This is how the story opens, as told in the King James Version.

> [19]There was a certain rich man, which was clothed in purple and fine linen, and fared sumptuously every day: [20]And there was a certain beggar named Lazarus, which was laid at his gate, full of sores, [21]And desiring to be fed with the crumbs which fell from the rich man's table: moreover the dogs came and licked his sores.

Then both men die and their positions somehow reverse.

> [2]And it came to pass, that the beggar died, and was carried by the angels into Abraham's bosom: the rich man also died, and was buried; [23]And in hell he lift up his eyes, being in torments, and seeth Abraham afar off, and Lazarus in his bosom.

Finally the rich man asks Abraham for a favor.

> [24]And he cried and said, Father Abraham, have mercy on me, and send Lazarus, that he may dip the tip of his finger in water, and cool my tongue; for I am tormented in this flame.

There you have it. Jesus says that the rich man dies, is in hell, and is in torment. The rich man seeks mercy because he is tormented in a flame. How could it be more obvious? With all this to work from, a sermon is not long in coming. When bad people die, the audience is assured, they go to hell where they are tormented in fire forever. And our authority is no less than Jesus himself.

But perhaps this conclusion is a bit hasty. For closer investigation reveals some interesting facts, as we will now observe.

31 THE RICH MAN AND LAZARUS (2)

Let's think through four details about this story Jesus told and be sure we are not about to misuse it ourselves. Those four details concern its form (parable, not history), its purpose (the context concerns subjects not related to final judgment and hell), its setting (here and now), and its intended mode (figurative or literal).

Parable, not factual narrative

The story of the rich man and Lazarus is not a factual narrative, but a borrowed parable. Parables usually teach one over-all lesson, sometimes two. The fact that Jesus used the parable does not mean that he endorsed all its details. Some object that this story cannot be a parable because it begins with the words "there was a certain rich man" and "there was a certain beggar."

In fact, it is just as likely that the quoted words mark the story *as* a parable. Two chapters later, Luke introduces another story with the words: "Now he told them a parable," leaving no doubt about the literary character of the story (Luke 18:1). Jesus then continues with the same kind of specific identification he uses in our story. "In a certain city there was a judge . . . and there was a widow in that city" (Luke 18:1-3). It is clear that mere specificity of detail does not mean a story is not a parable or that it is actually true.

In this case, the parable probably is not original with Jesus, but is one Jesus has borrowed from the rabbis. According to a 1966 doctoral dissertation, at least seven versions of this parable have been found in literature of the period.[15] Jesus simply borrows a tale from his surroundings, changing some details to make his point. This fact caused Robert A. Morey, a strong defender of the traditional view of hell, to conclude that this story does not provide us literal details of the world to come.[16]

Context concerns different subjects

Perhaps more important, if we read the Parable of the Rich Man and Lazarus in its context, we will see that the story's themes have nothing to do with hell or with the nature of final punishment. In Luke 16:1-13, Jesus teaches about the importance of stewardship. The Pharisees, who are covetous, mock Jesus and his teaching (Luke 16:14). Jesus warns the Pharisees that God sees the hearts and views people differently from their fellow mortals. He cautions that the times are critical and that people should not waste opportunity to obey God (Luke 16:15-18). Then Jesus tells this parable that illustrates all his points.

It is a story of a covetous man who ignores his responsibilities toward Lazarus as a steward of God's wealth. He is honored by people but God has a different view. And, after dying, the covetous man realizes too late that he has wasted his opportunity to obey God. The parable fits the context precisely and the themes they share in common reveal Jesus' purposes in telling this story.

Here and now, not future eternity

Besides all that, the details of this story occur here and now, not in eternity beyond the present age. While the rich man is agonizing in hades, his five brothers are still living on earth. I would like to say "living it up," but the text does not say that. However, the dead man seems to assume that his brothers view their possessions, as he also had done, in terms of *self* and not as God's possessions, entrusted to them to manage on God's behalf. It is all about *stewardship.*

Not only are the brothers still living during the present age, they live before Jesus' resurrection and while Moses and the prophets are God's latest word (Luke 16:29-31). This is important to the parable itself, because it sets up the story for its punch-line.

The rich man asks Abraham to send Lazarus to warn his five brothers. Abraham denies the request, saying they should listen to Moses and the prophets. The rich man replies that they would listen to someone who returned back from the dead. Abraham disagrees. If they ignore Moses and the prophets in Scriptures read weekly in synagogue, they will ignore someone back from the dead (Luke 16:27-31). Abraham proves to be correct. For Jesus himself will soon be killed, then rise from the dead, and the Pharisees who mock his teaching now will have the same attitude toward Jesus still.

But our eyes are on something different. In the story of the rich man and Lazarus, the action takes place *now*, not after judgment at the end of this age. People do not go to hell before they are judged. Final judgment happens after Jesus' final coming. The rich man in this story is not in *gehenna*, the place of final punishment. He is in *hades*, the unseen realm of the dead, the place called *sheol* in the Old Testament.

In fact, the "hell" in this story in the King James Version, the "hell" that has caught so many eyes and captured so many imaginations through the centuries, is not the hell of final punishment at all. It is simply *hades*, *sheol*, gravedom, the unseen realm of the dead. If the parable proved anything about post-mortem circumstances, it would still say nothing about final punishment in hell or *gehenna*.

Not literal

Finally, the parable should not be read literally, as if a literal reading contained Jesus' intended message. That would require one to believe:

- That Abraham receives the godly dead and remains with them;
- That angels transport the godly dead from earth to Abraham;
- That the godly and ungodly, though apart, are both audible and visible to each other;
- That a single drop of water would relieve the pain of the lost;
- That the saved can theoretically travel to the unsaved, or even to earth.

In fact, I have never met, heard, or read anyone who consistently interpreted the story of the rich man and Lazarus literally in every detail. It is not hard to understand why. The story of the rich man and Lazarus is a parable, not historical narrative. The context shows its subject something other than heaven and hell. Its setting is a time during ongoing earthly history and before Jesus is raised from the dead. And even if that were otherwise, it is not intended to be taken literally.

This is a story of the sort named "parable." It is a teaching tool about the urgency of obeying God in caring for the poor and a reminder that opportunity for doing that is running out. It says nothing at all about *gehenna*, the "hell" of final punishment. At most, this story is set in hades, before the judgment, while life on earth continues with its usual covetous ways.

Everlasting Torment: Pillar 3

NEW TESTAMENT WRITERS FOLLOW JESUS

Traditionalists say that New Testament writers follow Jesus, and therefore they also teach conscious unending torment.

---

32   JAMES, THE BROTHER OF JESUS

After Jesus was conceived in her womb without a biological human father, Mary later had at least four sons by Joseph, one of whom was named James. James was highly respected by Jesus' earliest follow-ers, who recognized him easily and early as an influential leader in the Jerusalem messianic community. James' short, practice-oriented epistle shares many points of similarity with Jesus' sayings in the Sermon on the Mount (Matt. 5-7) and provides an example of the earliest Jewish Christian teaching.

James' little book also illustrates the danger posed by unfounded expectations. The book of James never hints at unending torment, and it says much that sounds like total extinction. It is fair to say that James *stresses* future punishment—devoting one-third of his closing chapter to the subject—and that he speaks in *specifics*, not in *general thoughts*.

But notice what happens when a very fine scholar, who has been taught to associate "hell" with unending torment and never with total extinction, reads James. Not finding what he expected, and not expecting what he found, the very fine scholar goes away thinking that the book of James "does not put much stress on the doctrine of hell, though it does offer some general thoughts concerning the future punishment of the wicked."[17] How could the very fine scholar be so confused? The answer is simple. He was so busy listening for what James *did not* say that he failed to hear what James *did* say. It happens all the time.

According to James, the wicked are on a path to judgment and James describes its end five times. If the wicked continue in wickedness and refuse to repent, their destiny will be *death* (James 1:15) and *destruction* (4:12). Wealth that has been wrongfully acquired and sinfully hoarded will *consume* their flesh like *fire* (5:3). Too late they will realize that they have been fattened for the day of *slaughter* (5:5). Having gone full circle, James closes his book as he began: the end of the wicked is *death* (5:19).

33 WHERE DID HELL GO IN THE BOOK OF ACTS?

If any book of the Bible provides details about hell and the end of the wicked, surely that book is Acts of the Apostles. After all, Acts is *the* book about evangelism in the early church. Surely we can turn to Acts and read exciting details of exactly *how* "the early Christian evangelists and preachers . . . warned of the sure reality of hell and the eternal punishment of the unrepentant."[18]

That is what we would expect. Surprisingly, it is not what we find. We do find early Christian apostles, evangelists, and other disciples telling listeners across the Roman Empire about Jesus. God raised Jesus from the dead, they say. Through Jesus, anyone—Jews, Romans, people from all nations—can enjoy forgiveness of sins, receive God's Spirit, become children of God. But the message that rings most distinctly, as Acts reports the gospel's movement across the Greco-Roman world, is the offer of *life in Christ.*

What about *gehenna*, the "hell" of final punishment? It is never mentioned in Acts. Maybe it's listed under "Lake of Fire"? Not so. Perhaps graphic warnings of eternal torment? Not even once. Warnings of torment but not so graphic? Sorry. Still completely missing. One begins to suspect that the apostles motivated people with something better than fear. But there it is—feel free to check it out for yourself.

Acts begins with ten dozen disciples—men and women, apostles and vagabonds—frightened, hiding out in Jerusalem for fear of Jesus' enemies, waiting to be filled with supernatural power and boldness from heaven. The book ends with Paul under house arrest in Rome, eager to tell Caesar about Jesus, while from Jerusalem to Rome new Jesus-communities dot the landscape.

Does this mean that Peter and John and Paul ignored the alternative to eternal life? Were the earliest believers always silent about a day of judgment? Not at all. Such a conclusion is also unfounded. Here's the reality. In the whole book of Acts from start to finish, there are four clear references to final judgment or to the end of the wicked. Two texts reflect Peter's ministry and two reflect Paul's. We begin with Peter.

34 PETER'S PREACHING OF JUDGMENT

Acts of the Apostles reports two times when Peter specifically mentions either final judgment or final punishment. Once he is speaking to Gentiles and once to Jews.

A Gentile assembly

In Acts 10-11, Luke relates Peter's visit to Caesarea to preach the gospel at the household of a Roman centurion named Cornelius. Peter declares that God has set a day to judge the world. God has appointed Jesus Christ to act as judge in his stead and has confirmed the appointment by raising Jesus from the dead. This is the first specific mention in Acts of future judgment. Peter says nothing about the nature of final punishment here. His single reported comment on that subject had come much earlier, to an audience altogether different from the folks gathered at Cornelius' house.

A Jewish crowd

One day as Peter and John go to the Temple for afternoon prayers, they encounter a man lame from birth, whom God uses them to heal. A crowd quickly gathers, and Peter and John turn the conversation to Jesus, whom they credit for the healing. Jesus is the promised Messiah/Christ, the apostles say. He is also the prophet like Moses who was to come. And Moses himself prophesied that whoever does not listen to this prophet will be destroyed from among the people of God (Acts 3:22-23).

This is the only statement in Acts that describes or defines, even slightly, the nature of final punishment. And while the words *destroy* and *destruction* are among the most common words in the New Testament for the end of the unredeemed, in this text Luke uses a different Greek word for *destroy*, which appears only here in the New Testament. This is a very intense word that means "to destroy utterly" or "to root out."

But this word had a background—in the Septuagint (LXX), the Greek Old Testament of the Jews, the "Bible" quoted most often by Jesus and the early church. There the same Greek word translated "destroyed" in Acts 3:23 is regularly used to describe the effect of the Flood on the human population. And it is the ordinary word used in connection with the laws of capital punishment.

Is that ever a surprise!

35 PAUL'S PREACHING OF JUDGMENT

Acts contains two stories that include Paul's mention of final judgment and final punishment. As we listen to the first story, imagine yourself sitting in the marketplace in Athens, Greece, at a table, perhaps enjoying a huge, fresh Greek salad. (I did that once, and remember it still!)

The curious Athenians

Paul is in Athens on this particular day and he introduces the curious Greeks to a new God (Acts 17:22-31). But Paul claims that his *new* god is really the *original* God who made the universe. And instead of needing a caregiver to "heal" him—say, if his stone chin gets chipped and needs patching—this God gives life-breath to humans everywhere.

According to Paul, God made the nations and set their horizons in both time and space. Although invisible, God is always near. He longs for humankind to search for him, as if he were a friend gone missing. Then Paul suggests that these super-religious Greeks already acknowledge this God anonymously.

Presumably, when the Athenians were still filling their city with shrines to the gods, somebody anticipated a potential problem. What if they accidentally overlooked a deity—and this deity happened to be intolerant of mortals who make honest mistakes. Anyone who has read classical mythology knows the wisdom of not getting at odds with fickle Greek gods.

So, just to be safe, they dedicated one shrine to *AGNOSTO THEO*—"A God Unknown." But today the God whom they *did not know* has sent his messenger Paul to tell them what they *need to know.* And Paul's message that day begins by saying that *not knowing* is no longer an excuse.

God demands a change in thinking, which is repentance, Paul says. He has set a day when he will judge the world in justice, through the man Jesus. God himself appointed Jesus, and to make that clear to everyone, God raised Jesus from the dead (Acts 17:30-31).

Everybody who heard Paul talk that day knew one thing for sure. His message was nothing like the usual Aeropagus philosophy and chatter. Paul's message had strange power and themes equally strange to Athenian minds. This Jew who was a Roman citizen and who also spoke Greek had said, for example . . .

God will judge the world. People are accountable. Actions have consequences and choices matter. Greek gods do not judge Greek people, much less the whole world. In most cases, the gods of the Greeks would never make it through judgment themselves.

God's judgment will be just. Each person will be held accountable for the response to God's light received and for the use of opportunities granted. Morality and justice will clearly be on the same side. Every punishment will fit the crime. Whatever happens in God's courtroom, all present will go away saying that the outcome was correct. Nobody will think that God's justice is unfair or that it needs defending.

God has appointed Jesus Christ to be judge. The more Paul says about his God and the message that God has given Paul to tell the nations, the clearer it becomes that everything is finally about Jesus Christ.

God raised Jesus from the dead. Paul's closing remarks about someone named "Jesus," obviously a non-Greek foreigner, likely a rural individual, held no appeal to most of the Athenians. But then matters got even worse. Raising someone from the dead? What a vulgar concept! Why would anyone *want* such a future as that? What will these Jews think up next?

The Athenians prefer the wisdom of Socrates, who lived and taught four centuries earlier, roughly contemporaneous with Paul's Hebrew prophet Malachi. Socrates did more than talk. He demonstrated by his own example how a truly wise philosopher welcomes death and the unshackling of the soul from the mortal, earth-bound body.

Socrates' disciple Plato constantly reminded his pupils that, although the mortal body dies and returns to dust, the *psyche* or soul is immortal and will live somewhere forever. What need does such beautiful philosophy have for the resurrection of the body?

Mixed-motive Felix

Our second story involving Paul takes place approximately six or seven years later. Paul has been arrested in Jerusalem and transferred to Caesarea to appear before the Roman governor Felix. Hoping for a bribe, Felix leaves Paul in prison for two years until he himself is replaced by Porcius Festus.

During this time, Felix "often" sends for Paul and argues with him about "justice and self-control and future judgment" (Acts 24:25-27). This text confirms that judgment was a topic of conversation, but it tells us nothing about Paul's description of judgment or of the nature of final punishment.

36   PAUL'S WRITINGS

In one sense, Paul says more about hell than anyone else in the Bible. Rather remarkable, since he never uses the word "hell" even once.

That raises an interesting question. If Paul does not use the word "hell," yet still says the most about it, what kind of language does he use to talk about the final end of the wicked? Earlier, I mentioned that the three words used most often in the New Testament outside the Gospels are *die, perish,* and *destroy.*

The following paragraphs include a number of key words that Paul uses to describe the final destiny of the unredeemed. Although Paul does not use the word *gehenna* (the "hell" of final punishment), we can accurately say that these words listed below tell what Paul believed will happen to those who go to hell.

Paul says the wicked will *not inherit the kingdom.* The point is so important that Paul mentions it in three different epistles (1 Cor. 6:9-10; Gal. 5:21; Eph. 5:5). The redeemed will enjoy an everlasting paradise in new heavens and new earth. Those who go to hell will never enjoy a single moment of God's eternal kingdom.

They will not have even one glimpse of the city of God, a city so beautiful it is described as having golden streets, jeweled walls, and gates of pearl. They will never taste the tree of life. They will suffer the loss of every good thing that is, and every beautiful thing that might have been.

The wicked will not enjoy any of God's blessings that the redeemed enjoy, because they will *perish* (Rom. 2:12). They are *anathema*, which means *marked for destruction* (1 Cor. 16:22; Gal. 1:8-9). This is not some theoretical statement that might really happen and might not. No, God will *destroy* them (Rom. 2:12; 1 Cor. 3:17). Paul says it every way he can say it. The wicked will suffer *destruction* (Gal. 5:20; 6:8; Phil. 1:28; 3:19). That destruction will be *sudden* when it comes (1 Thess. 5:3), and, once accomplished, it will be *everlasting* (2 Thess. 1:9).

But that does not mean the destruction will happen instantaneously. The destructive process will include *distress* (Rom. 2:9), *fury* (Rom. 2:8), *tribulation* (Rom. 2:9) and God's *wrath* (Rom. 2:8; 1 Thess. 1:10; 5:9). No one should think that the wicked will simply go quietly asleep. This is not an easy demise. The second death is not a peaceful death.

These words that Paul commonly uses to describe the end of the wicked—words such as *die* and *death, perish,* and *destroy* and *destruction*—are some of the strongest, most vivid words available to Paul to tell his churches what will happen to the wicked.

It is strange beyond understanding how anyone can read these words in Paul's epistles and explain them to mean anything other than total *extinction,* unending *cessation,* and complete *annihilation.* Not only does Paul use such strong clear language, there is every reason to believe that he chose these very words because they are so strong.

When we read in the New Testament that the wicked finally *die, perish,* and are *destroyed,* we are reading these words in a context and often with a contrast. The *context* is a public conversation that had been going since about the time of Malachi—which also happened to be about the time of Socrates and Plato. After Socrates had drunk the poisonous hemlock and was waiting for it to take effect, he conversed with his friends and students about death and the attitude proper for a philosopher regarding death.

Plato later recreated or invented a dialogue that supposedly represented what Socrates and his companions said on that occasion, and that dialog later was published as the *Phaedo*. Some people in the conversation argued that when a man dies, his body and soul *die, perish,* and are *destroyed.* When they said this, they used the same Greek words that Paul and other New Testament writers used when they said that the wicked (but not the redeemed) will *die, perish,* and be *destroyed.*

Others in the conversation argued that when a man dies, his body *dies, perishes,* and is *destroyed,* but that his soul is immortal and cannot *die, perish,* or be *destroyed.* When they said this, they used the same Greek words that Paul and other New Testament writers used when they said that the wicked (but not the redeemed) will *die, perish,* and be *destroyed.*

It would make no sense at all to give the words *die, perish,* and be *destroyed* a meaning in the New Testament that they did not have in everyday conversation. These words belong to a context within an ongoing conversation.

The natural meaning of words such as *die, perish,* and be *destroyed* is strengthened even more when these words are used in *contrasts* with words that mean the opposite. For example, Paul writes to the Roman believers that the wages of sin is *death.* In contrast, he says the gift of God is *eternal life.*

The options are life and death. The contrast makes it clear that the *death* the wicked will experience in hell is the opposite of *life.* It is non-life. It is *death* in the usual meaning of the word— now enlarged to its fullest capacity and packed with meaning. As Jesus warns, God can destroy both soul and body forever.

37 HEBREWS: Traitors beware

No one knows who wrote Hebrews or to whom, or when, or where, or exactly why. From what it says, we conclude that its original readers were second or third-generation believers. They are suffering a faith crisis, for which the text hints at a variety of possible causes. The list might include verbal abuse from associates, confiscation of property, and temporary imprisonment.

The author of Hebrews appeals to their best instincts as he urges them to remain faithful to Jesus. Most of all, he says, Jesus also suffered, but he endured even death and remained faithful to God. God then showed himself to be faithful to the one who is faithful to him. He raised Jesus from the dead and gave him the place of highest honor at his right hand in heaven.

According to the unknown author of Hebrews, the person who has professed belief in Jesus and later abandons faith is a traitor who deserves severe punishment. Worse than physical death alone (2:2-3), the punishment appropriate to crass faithlessness is like the fate of barren ground that is cursed and burned (6:8). We are speaking of destruction (10:39), as if in a raging (10:27-31), consuming fire (12:29).

The author of Hebrews, like other biblical writers before him, speaks in symbols and figures of speech. We must take him seriously but not literally. Doing that, we ask again the question we have asked about other biblical authors. Reading everything that he has said, which kind of fire seems most consistent with the warnings in Hebrews? Is it the fire that *torments endlessly,* the fire that *purifies,* or is it the fire that *consumes?*

38   BEWARE OF COUNTERFEITS: 2 Peter & Jude

We visited the small books called 2 Peter and Jude already, when we considered the Flood and Sodom's annihilation as prototypes or examples of the punishment at the end of the world. The middle chapter (chapter 2) of 2 Peter and the single chapter in Jude are very much alike. Jude is a brother of James who also wrote a New Testament book and, like James, is a half-brother of Jesus. Second Peter presents itself as the work of Peter the apostle, who wrote 1 Peter.

Both 2 Peter 2 and Jude 1 are stern warnings against certain teachers who claimed to represent an advanced form of Christianity. Their "advanced" morality says that God's grace shines more brightly the more flagrantly believers sin. The natural result of such teaching is to encourage believers to sin more wildly to stir up more grace.

But Peter and Jude will have none of this "advanced" gospel. It is a perversion of grace, not an advanced form of grace (2 Pet. 2:2; Jude 4). They also have no patience for those who teach it. Peter and Jude see these teachers as counterfeit Christians, fraudulent fakes, who will mislead God's people if they are not exposed first. The false teachers are hell-bound, according to both 2 Peter and Jude.

Second Peter says the bad teachers face "swift destruction" (2 Peter 2:1) and "condemnation" (2:3). If anyone does not think God judges evil, that person should remember the destruction of Sodom and Gomorrah in Abraham's day. These twin cities were turned into ashes, Peter says, when God made them an example of what will happen to the wicked at the end of the world (2:6). Jude comments that the cities are an example of the punishment of eternal fire (Jude 7).

Second Peter also points to fallen angels now imprisoned in gloomy darkness waiting for judgment (2:4). Some translations say these angels are in "hell," but that is misleading. Second Peter says "Tartarus," a location in Homer's "Odyssey." It does not say *gehenna,* the New Testament's "hell" of final punishment. Even if this text said *gehenna,* it would not add to our knowledge, because it concerns angels and not humans, at a time before the judgment and not after it.

Second Peter says the false teachers will "perish" like brute beasts that are caught and "destroyed" (2:12). This reminds us of James comparing the evil person's going to hell to a fattened animal's "day of slaughter" (James 5:5).

Second Peter and Jude now move their gaze from the earth to the heavens. In the end, the wicked will experience what we call "black holes" in outer space (2:17; Jude 13). Both men describe it as "blackest darkness." Jude adds the detail of "wandering stars." Total darkness graphically symbolizes fading into non-existence, like some wayward star swallowed by a hyper-gravity black hole.

Second Peter points to the Flood as a preview of final punishment. Just as the old world and its people perished by water in the past, so wicked people will be destroyed by fire in the future (2:5-7). It is obvious what *perish* and *destroy* mean when describing the effects of the Flood. The meanings are no less plain when the same words are used about final punishment.

In closing, Jude admonishes his readers to care for each other. By God's love and mercy, the destiny of believers will be eternal life (Jude 21). But to arrive at that goal, some need to be rescued from time to time. Jude describes the act of rescuing as snatching someone from the fire (Jude 22). The imagery comes from Amos 4:11. There the prophet Amos compares a remnant of people returned home from exile to a stick pulled from a fire just before it bursts into flame and burns up.

39   JOHN: Life or death

It has been traditionally understood that John the Apostle wrote the Gospel of John, the epistles 1 John, 2 John, 3 John, and Revelation. For our purposes here, we will assume that to be correct. If it is not, what we say below is still true, only of several authors instead of one.

Throughout the Gospel of John, Jesus speaks most often of the final state of the saved as "eternal life" (John 3:16). On the other hand, John repeatedly states that the unredeemed will *die, perish,* and be *destroyed.* Even now, the willful disbeliever lives under the shadow of divine *wrath*—as if covered constantly by the wings of a giant bird of prey (John 3:36).

John writes of a sin that results in "death" (1 John 5:16-17). We commonly speak of people who are killed in an accident or natural catastrophe as *perishing.* For that reason, we are not surprised when John speaks of the alternative to life as being to "perish" (John 3:16). The same end is in view when Revelation warns that God will "destroy" those who destroy the earth (Rev.11:18).

In fact, those three words—*die, perish,* and be *destroyed*—are the very words that New Testament writers use most often to describe the final end of the wicked. Isn't it interesting that most modern believers think they are sure that those who go to hell will *not* die, will *never* perish, and certainly will *never* be destroyed.

40   THE LAKE OF FIRE INTRODUCED

Several times the Book of Revelation mentions the "lake of fire and brimstone" or "the fiery lake of burning sulfur." What does this symbolic scene with the puzzling name represent? We remember first that the visual image of "fire and brimstone" is a picture based on the annihilation of Sodom and Gomorrah. The Bible does not specifically say that God destroyed these cities with volcanic eruptions. However, the description in Genesis sounds like that is exactly what happened. That is the image we see whenever we read the words "fire and brimstone."

Fiery river/lake

Now John sees a vision. In the vision he sees a lake. But the lake is not filled with water. It is filled with fire and burning sulfur. This horrible lake is not pictured anywhere in the Bible outside of the Book of Revelation. However, if we search diligently, we can find a vision in the Old Testament very much like this vision of John's.

That earlier vision is recorded in Daniel 7, where it is part of a larger story the prophet saw. Like John much later, Daniel sees an image of God's heavenly throne. The throne is central and the one sitting on it controls the whole universe. He did in Daniel's day. He still did in John's day. He remains in charge today.

Flowing out from the throne, Daniel sees a river of fire. Instead of a fiery *river*, John sees a *lake* of fire. These two sights are easily smaller views of the same larger scene. Just as the Jordan River flows into the sea called the Dead Sea where nothing lives, this river of fire flows into the lake of fire which is the second death and where nothing is alive.

Daniel's beastly narrative

Daniel sees four beasts, creatures representing world powers that oppose God's authority and his kingdom. But no matter how powerful these opponents of God might be, they are finally no match for God. That is the message in the video story written in symbols that God showed to Daniel.

In Daniel's vision, the first three beasts are stripped of authority and finally destroyed. The fourth beast, more powerful and terrible than the others, is killed. Its dead body is destroyed in the blazing fire. These opponents who once stood in God's way are defeated, destroyed, and finally gone. Beasts lose. God wins.

The details of the fourth beast's demise emphasize its destruction. There is no possibility that we will see it again later when we least expect to. This fourth beast will not suddenly reappear or revive or rise up alive, like something in a Hollywood horror movie. Daniel sees it *killed*. Its body is *destroyed*—tossed into the *blazing fire*. This beast is no more. It will never be a threat to anything or to anyone again.

John's beastly narrative

In Revelation, John sees a vision much like Daniel's. John also sees strange beings and symbolic beasts that represent world powers in opposition to God's authority and his kingdom. The rebel leader is the devil (Satan). The devil's chief officer is called Beast. Beast symbolizes every human government that claims authority higher than God's, requires its citizens to agree with that, and persecutes (even kills) anyone who refuses.

From the first century onward, there have been governments that fit this description. First there was Imperial Rome. More recent centuries have seen such governments under Hitler, Stalin, Mao Zedong, Pol Pot, and others.

Knowing these things, whenever any government begins to claim an authority higher than God's, believers do well to hear an alarm—a loudspeaker that shouts a single word of warning: *Beast!*

Beast's cohort is False Prophet. From earliest human history until today, governments have enjoyed having the support of religion. The ancient Babylonians built ziggurats with temples at the top for their gods to visit. The ancient Egyptians believed that their Pharaoh ("king" in Egyptian) was the son of the Sun-god *Re*.

But governments and religion are dangerous comrades. They have a strong tendency to believe in themselves above everything else. They have a habit of exalting themselves, then forcing others to exalt them also.

Knowing these things, whenever believers face a partnership that claims to represent both God and government, those believers do well to hear an alarm—a loudspeaker that shouts two words of warning: *False Prophet!*

But no matter how powerful these opponents of God might be, they are finally no match for God. As with Daniel, this is also the message in the video story written in symbols that God showed to John. In John's vision also, all the opponents who stood in God's way are defeated, destroyed, and finally gone. Rebels lose. God wins.

There is no possibility that we will see the rebel crowd again. These creatures will not suddenly reappear or revive when we least expect it. No. When John's vision ends, rebels are gone forever. Devil, Beast, and False Prophet are all in the lake of fire. They will never be a threat to anything or to anyone again.

41 UNHOLY TRIO MEET THE LAKE OF FIRE

Near the end of his symbol-filled vision, John hears a great triumphant chorus of voices from heaven announcing God's victory and the vindication of his faithful people. Heaven is opened and John sees a heavenly army riding on white horses. Leading them on a majestic white horse is Jesus Christ, the King over all earthly kings (Rev. 19:11-21). At this point in the video, the narrative includes symbolic words and phrases taken from Old Testament prophecies—symbols that tell us that Jesus is coming to judge the nations.

But the rebel forces in apparent control of earth do not surrender quietly. In the video, John sees Beast and the kings of earth with their armies making preparation for one final counter-attack. Their efforts are futile. The battle is over as soon as it begins.

The forces of heaven capture Beast and False Prophet, and throw them alive into the Lake of Fire. The rebel armies, now without their leader (Beast) and his cohort (False Prophet), are all slaughtered by the sword that comes out of Jesus' mouth (Rev.19:12-21). The war is over, although one battle still remains. Beast and False Prophet are in the Lake of Fire. We will see them once more.

The Old Testament prophet Ezekiel foretold the ultimate battle between God and rebel forces called "Gog" and "Magog" (Ezek. 38-39). Satan's armies surround the camp of God's people for a final assault. The scene reminds us of the battle for Helm's Deep in J.R.R. Tolkien's *Lord of the Rings*—which, of course, Tolkien based on symbols in Ezekiel and in Revelation. But just as the rebels suppose that they have prevailed, fire comes down from heaven and toasts them in their tracks (Rev. 20:7-10).

In John's video, Satan is pictured as thrown into the Lake of Fire, joining Beast and False Prophet. There the three rebel leaders—the unholy trinity—the mirror image of all that is good and just and true—will remain. In the video of symbols, these three "are tormented day and night forever and ever."

This is the only text in the whole Bible that speaks of anything being tormented forever. The statement applies to the devil, Beast, and False Prophet, neither of which is a human being. Scripture nowhere says that any human being will be tormented forever. Jesus does say the wicked will suffer "eternal punishment" (Matt. 25:46), which Paul explains to be "eternal destruction" (2 Thess. 1: 9).

Perhaps one knows best the intended meaning of Scripture who stands most nearly in the shoes of the person or people for whom it was first written. Hanns Lilje was one of several Christian pastors and authors imprisoned by Hitler's Gestapo—Dietrich Bonhoeffer is perhaps the best-known. Just as John saw Beast close-up and encountered False Prophet, so did Lilje (and Bonhoeffer) nearly nineteen centuries later.

Hermann L. Strack and Paul Billerbeck say that in the symbol-language of that time even everlasting torment can symbolize everlasting, irreversible extinction.[19] Lilje certainly would concur. On this passage in Revelation, he writes: "God's will has triumphed gloriously; the 'lake of fire' means no more than this."[20]

42 DEATH AND HADES ANNIHILATED

The lake of fire is not yet full. However, we are not yet out of candidates, either.

Death

Tossed next into the fire in John's symbol-language vision is Death itself (Rev. 20:14). This is death as we know it, death as humans have always known it. Death is not a living being, of course. It is the *absence* of life. Indeed, death is the exact *opposite* of life. These are the two final options for humans. It is either *life* (eternal life at that!) or *death* (the second, final, everlasting death).

It should be obvious that life and death cannot coexist. Someone is either dead or alive. The same person is not both dead and alive at the same time. These two final options are stated clearly in Romans 6:23, where the wages of sin is *death*, but the gift of God is *eternal life*.

As we come to the close of the Book of Revelation, we meet these two final options again. At the end, we see humankind divided into two groups identified by these two words: *life* (represented by the Book of Life) and *death* (represented by the Lake of Fire).

Both the Old Testament (Isa. 25:7-8) and the New Testament (1 Cor. 15:54) look forward to a time when Death will no longer exist anywhere. During his visual trip into the future, John sees that time arrive.

Whatever they think about the end of human beings, scholars on all sides of the hell debate agree concerning the meaning of the picture in Revelation 20:14, the video clip showing Death tossed into the Lake of Fire. No one disputes that this is symbol-language standing for the annihilation, the extinction, the very "death" of Death. The English poet John Donne was correct when he exclaimed: "Death shall be no more; Death, thou shalt die."[21]

Hades

When Death is thrown into the Lake of Fire, Hades is also thrown in. *Hades* is a Greek word that literally means *the unseen realm.* In the Old Testament, Hades is called by the name *Sheol*—pictured as the abode of the dead. Some writers have argued that Sheol is the same as hell, the place of final punishment. Others claim that Sheol or Hades is the first stage of final Hell. Based on Old Testament comments about Sheol, the wisest way to understand Hades is simply as a symbol for the invisible realm of the dead. To say more than that becomes very troublesome when one recalls that Jesus is pictured as in Hades (or Sheol) between his death and his resurrection (Acts 2:27, 31).

When Death is gone, so will be the place or state of the dead. That is Hades or Sheol—which is also cast into the Lake of Fire (Rev.20:14). Again, all sides in the debate about hell agree that the time will come when Hades also will become extinct, no longer in existence. For Hades to be thrown into the Lake of Fire simply means its total and everlasting destruction. It is annihilated. It will never be seen again.

43   THE LAKE OF FIRE IS HUMAN SECOND DEATH

John twice mentions human beings thrown into the Lake of Fire. Both times, he adds the explanatory words: "which is the second death." John begins by naming the symbol to be defined—"the Lake of Fire." He then defines that symbol by equating it with a different reality easy to be understood—"the second death." What is the *Lake of Fire?* It is the symbol of something, but what does it symbolize?

What it is, is . . .

The answer is not self-evident, so John explains. The Lake of Fire *is* the second death. The first death is the death we experience now in the present age. It is temporary—the redeemed will be raised from it to immortality and resurrection glory.

The second death is the death of the age to come, the death from which God rescues those who believe in Jesus. The second death is the death that is the wages of sin. It is the destruction and perishing promised to the unfaithful. It is the death from which there is no resurrection or return. It is the death of the whole person forever.

The *second death* is the reality, easily understood. It is *represented* by the more difficult *symbol*—the *Lake of Fire.* By defining his expression this way, John encourages and invites us to think of the reality when we encounter its symbol. So we see the name *Lake of Fire* (unclear symbol) and think *the second death* (clearer reality).

Because John defined the *Lake of Fire* as *the second death,* we are not free to reason the other direction. We do not have John's permission to explain *the second death* as the *Lake of Fire,* which would be moving from the simpler to the more difficult. We follow John, however, each time we define the symbol "Lake of Fire" as "the second death."

Registry of the living / Second death

The first reference to humans being tossed into the Lake of Fire identifies the lake as one of two final destinies. The other destiny is life in the City of God, symbolized as registration in the Book of Life. Every human being finally goes to one destiny or the other. Either one's name is written in the Book of Life or one is thrown into the Lake of Fire which is the second death (Rev. 20:15). The comparison is strong: *life* or *death.*

The images are vivid. The Book of Life is a registry of the living citizens in a particular city. When a resident dies, his or her name is removed from the city's book of living citizens. When a new baby is born to a resident family, a new name is written in the Book of Life. In Revelation, the Book of Life is the registry of those who live forever in the New Jerusalem.

The other option is the Lake of Fire. At this point in the text, this Lake has received Beast, False Prophet, Satan, Death, and Hades. Now the second reference to humans in the Lake of Fire describes the character of people who go there (Rev. 21:8). The traits begin with *cowardly* and *faithless* and they end with *all liars.*

Viewed together from a modest distance, these attributes and others named between them present the classic portrait of a traitor, a betrayer. This is someone who claims to be Jesus' disciple when times are good. But when opposition comes and pressure builds, he changes loyalties, flips sides, and denies the Lord and Savior.

These are the only two references in the Bible to human beings going into the Lake of Fire. Both times, John explains the meaning of the Lake of Fire by adding the words: "which is the second death."

Both Old and New Testaments picture new heavens and new earth, an eternal universe forever free of all sin, without temptation, where everything in creation praises and worships God (Isa. 24:14-16; 2 Pet. 3:13). It is impossible to harmonize that picture with another picture that shows most humans who ever lived, screaming and writhing day and night in a place of everlasting conscious torment as they suffer unspeakable pain forever.

Some today who argue that the damned will suffer pain forever now claim that language as used in the previous sentence misrepresents the tradition. These advocates say that the pains suffered by the lost are more intellectual and less physical than was previously thought.

To any who claim misrepresentation, I recommend a course of regular reading from the sermons of John Chrysostom, John Wesley, Charles Spurgeon, Jonathan Edwards, and A. W. Pink.

It is also impossible to square the traditional doctrine of hell—which says that God will actively keep most of the entire human race alive forever for the sole purpose of tormenting them without end—with statements throughout the Bible that teach the final extinction of the wicked: the total, irreversible annihilation of the whole person.

Is one supposed to conclude that dozens, even scores and more of simple, declaratory statements throughout all of Scripture must finally be ignored because of fewer than five symbolic verses in Revelation? It makes far better sense to read these few apocalyptic statements written in symbolic language in light of the clear, repeated, consistent teaching from throughout all the rest of Scripture.

44   PERSONAL STRUGGLE

As mentioned earlier, I began my year-long research assignment by reading every book I could find in defense of the traditional view. Then I read the books that taught the extinction of the lost. Using Scripture references from all these books as starters, I worked through the entire Bible seeking the only inspired light we have on this subject.

I was amazed to find that the Old Testament, which traditionalists assured me held nothing of interest or value on the subject of final punishment, instead proved to be a treasure-house of information. The supposed silence of the Old Testament on this topic was the first pillar of traditionalism, and its total falsity left me feeling disappointed but also betrayed. Those same two feelings would become familiar callers throughout the course of my research.

One by one, the pillars of traditionalism crumbled at my touch, like paper burnt to ash just waiting to disintegrate. It is no exaggeration to say that much I expected to find in the Bible was *not* there, and most of what I *did* find in Scripture was a total surprise. This raised another question: If the traditional view is not found in the Bible, where did it come from? I found that answer in Tertullian and the supposed immortality of the soul.

One final question pounded my brain without mercy, intensifying the ongoing inward struggle. Should I write a book, bringing into the bright light of day all the biblical truths I personally had encountered in the form of earth-shaking, ground-breaking surprises? Could I write that book? Dare I write that book?

To this point in my life, I had always held to the traditional view of everlasting torment. I fully expected to hold it for the remainder of my life as well. Despite the questions that most sensitive believers sometimes ask, I had no passion to change views. All I wanted was to understand what God has revealed on the subject and to teach it to others to the glory of God. In terms of personal comfort, I had absolutely nothing to gain by changing. On the other hand, changing views on hell—especially publicly—carried considerable risk.

If I rejected the traditional view of everlasting torment, I would be going against the overwhelming majority of the Christian church for at least 1,600 years. It would place me at odds with my own Christian faith tradition in the Stone-Campbell Restoration Movement. It would mean rejecting what my father had believed and taught. He had died about seven years before, but my love, respect, and near reverence for him continued as it does until this day.

I already had a reputation among the hard-liners on the fringes of our fellowship as an iconoclast. The thought of becoming permanently suspect or worse among the mainstream as well held very little appeal to a young preacher with a tenuous and unknown future.

Besides all that, to reject the traditional view in favor of "annihilationism" or "conditional immortality," as this other view was known, would mean agreeing with the Seventh-day Adventists on this issue. That fact alone was enough to condemn the view in the minds of many.

I had argued at length with the Adventists on this very topic when I took their *Voice of Prophecy* correspondence courses as a teenager—along with courses from the Knights of Columbus, the Rosicrucians, the Worldwide Church of God, our own Churches of Christ, and perhaps others as well. Critics would taunt that I had regressed in understanding rather than growing wiser.

But there was another consideration more substantial than all the others combined. It was a guiding principle that had characterized my parents and my mother's parents who devoted their lives to preaching the gospel in Africa. This was one of the earliest lessons I had learned from my father, and I pray it will go with me into eternity. One can state it many ways but the essence is the same: "If the Bible says it, it's true, no matter what any person may say."

By the grace of God, I had studied the Bible since childhood, and had attended Athens Bible School from grades one through twelve. I had a graduate degree in biblical languages. I was trained to analyze Scripture (a task called *exegesis*), to interpret it (*hermeneutics*), and to apply it to every-day life (*homiletics*). While preaching in St. Louis, I had read systematic and historical theology in two seminaries—one conservative (Covenant) and one liberal (Eden).

Might it be, I wondered, that God had been preparing me for this very time? I had done the research. I had used the tools and used them properly. Throughout it all, I had prayed for guidance. Christian brothers and sisters were praying for me every day of the research, at home in the Barn church and all around the world. What more could anyone do? Now I needed to trust the results. Despite the high risks and the potential costs, my course was clear. Straight ahead!

45   REFRESHING OUR MEMORIES

We have now explored our way through the whole Bible from Genesis to Revelation, asking one question of everyone we met. "What can you tell us about the final state of the unredeemed?" From beginning to end, the answer has come back loud and clear. "The wages of sin is *death.*"

In the Old Testament, we learned from principles, previews and predictions. We discovered *principles of divine justice*—righteousness is rewarded, evil is punished. If it does not happen in this life, it will happen later. Rebellious sinners cannot escape God's justice. The psalmists describe what that will look like, using at least seventy similes and metaphors and at least fifty Hebrew verbs.

Two of the best-known stories in Genesis are in fact *previews of divine judgment.* The Flood in Noah's day and the annihilation of Sodom and Gomorrah were total devastations. In the first story, no breathing life remained outside the Ark; in the second story nothing was left but smoke. The New Testament says both events exemplify the fate awaiting the wicked at the end of the world.

Old Testament prophets also provide specific *predictions of the wicked's end.* They paint a variety of word pictures. But whether the picture features a sword, or smoke, or fire and maggots, the pictures all mean the same—death and total destruction.

As we move through the New Testament with our same question, we hear many voices. John the Baptist announces, Jesus tells parables, evangelists proclaim, apostles and others write epistles, and John sees mysterious and symbolic visions. Again, many methods but a single message: the time will come when the wicked will no longer exist.

When New Testament writers describe the future of those who throughout life reject God, the three words they use the most are *die* (or *death), perish,* and *destroy* (or *destruction*). Often these words are used in direct contrast to *eternal life* that awaits the saved. The final options could not be stated more plainly. The choices are *life* or *death*. The Bible never says that any human being will be kept alive forever to suffer everlasting conscious torment in hell.

According to the New Testament, the wicked will not live forever for two reasons: one positive and one negative. The positive reason is expressed in the words of destruction noted above. The consequences of sin are to die, to perish, to be destroyed. The negative reason is grounded in the fact that human beings are totally dependent creatures who exist only because God made them, and who will continue to exist only if God enables them and gives them life.

Scripture is clear that only God possesses immortality (1 Tim. 6:16). He alone lives eternally and is his own source of life. God's life does not depend on anyone other than himself. That cannot be said of any creature in the universe, including us human beings. For us, immortality is God's free gift to the redeemed (Rom. 2:6-8). We live in hope of "the promise of the life that is in Christ" (2 Tim. 1:1).

The Bible says nothing of immortal souls. Instead, it tells a story of God making man from dust of the earth. "Then the LORD God formed man of *dust* from the ground, and breathed into his nostrils the *breath of life*; and man became a *living being*" (Gen 2:7). The King James Version said that man became a "living soul," which modern versions improve with "living being" (the same Hebrew word is also used of the animals). And even in the King James Version, man was not *given* a "living soul" (like another "part"). He *became* a "living soul" or a holistic living being.

We humans are dependent creatures, having no life-source in our natural selves. We are wholly mortal, destined to die, and—unless God intervenes—to stay dead. But the Bible tells us that God *will* intervene. He will raise all the dead to be judged. God will transform the bodies of the redeemed and make them *immortal* (1 Cor. 15:54-57).

The wicked also will be raised—not immortal, but to the resurrection of condemnation (John 5:28-29). They will face God, be condemned and banished to hell, the lake of fire. There they will *perish* (John 3:16), be *destroyed* both soul and body (Matt. 10:28). In the process, they will suffer conscious pains precisely in keeping with divine justice—not more, not less. To say it another way, they suffer the *second death* (Rev. 21:8). They suffer the *eternal punishment* of *eternal destruction* (Matt. 25:46; 2 Thess. 1:9).

But this raises some other interesting questions. If the traditional view of everlasting torment does not originate in the Bible, where does it come from? And, if it is not the view set out in Scripture, how did it become so popular and why is it held by almost everyone even today?

46 TERTULLIAN:
Plato joins the church

From the closing of the first century through the first three-quarters of the second century come the writings of those called the "apostolic fathers." When they speak of final punishment, they use the same biblical language of life and death that we saw throughout the Bible itself. Likely written for use as a manual for new believers, the Didache is unmistakable about final options. "There are two ways," it begins, "the way of life and the way of death." Ignatius of Antioch reminds the Magnesians, a church not mentioned in the New Testament, that "two things lie before us, life and death."

Tertullian

During the second and third centuries after Christ, a number of pagan philosophers became Christians and devoted their talents to reasoning with non-Christian thinkers. Chief among them was a man from Carthage, a fiery-tempered philosopher named Tertullian. He was a convert from the followers of Socrates and Plato, who believed that every human being had a mortal body and an immortal soul.

According to Socrates, his pupil Plato, and others after them, humans have two "parts"—a mortal body that dies and an immortal soul that by its very nature cannot die. Of the two, Socrates said, the soul is nobler and far more significant. It is eternal, existing before the body, and being immortal, it survives the body's death.

Tertullian was practically obsessed with thoughts of the soul. He wrote his longest book on the subject. For proof that the soul is immortal, the church father appealed to Plato. In a work titled "Resurrection of the Flesh," Tertullian wrote: "I may use, therefore, the opinion of Plato, when he declares, 'Every soul is immortal.'" Because the soul is immortal already, Tertullian reasoned, it does not need saving. Christ came to save only the body.

But most important to our inquiry is Tertullian's reasoning about the immortal soul and hell. When Jesus warns that God can *destroy* the soul (Matt. 10:28), we should not think of *destruction*, said Tertullian, for immortal souls cannot be destroyed. Jesus really means that the soul will suffer conscious punishment in hell. Through Tertullian's influence, we might say, pagan Plato joined the Christian church.

The assumption was wrong but the logic was straight and simple. If souls are truly "immortal," they cannot *die, perish,* or be *destroyed*—the three words used most often in the Bible to describe the final end of the wicked. And if they will never die but live forever, there are but two possibilities: either the souls of the wicked live forever in torment or they are eventually purified and graduate to heaven. The church fathers were never consistent about the destructibility of the soul, always acknowledging that God is able to destroy whatever he creates, but reasoning about hell as if that were not the case.

A few years later, Origen of Alexandria would propose universal "restoration," an explanation growing in popularity again today. But the overwhelming view of the church—the view that became orthodoxy for Catholics and Protestants alike—was everlasting conscious torment.

Scripture does speak of human immortality, to be sure. But when it does, three things are always true, and three things are never true. These details are set out graphically in the diagram below. Please review it carefully. I encourage you to take out your best concordance and look up every passage in the New Testament that uses the words "mortality" and "immortality" or "mortal" or "immortal." Test the statements in the diagram below by comparing them with every verse that uses any of those words.

HUMAN IMMORTALITY IN THE BIBLE		
Always		**But Never**
Who?	the saved	the lost
What?	the whole person	a disembodied soul or spirit
When?	the resurrection	at birth or at the new birth

These truths are so important that if the church had always remembered them, the idea of everlasting conscious torment probably never would have arisen at all. If that idea had appeared in a church that remembered these three truths, the idea would have been soundly rejected.

Clement and Origen

Clement and Origen were successive headmasters of a famous school in Alexandria, Egypt, known for its allegorical interpretation of the Scriptures. Both men are also known by their name with the added suffix, "of Alexandria." They lived into the third century. Clement and later Origen reasoned that God does everything for a reason. Hell's reason, they speculated, was to purify the soul and prepare the soul for heaven. This theory they called the *Apokatastasis* or Restoration, and it added a third purpose for hell's fire in addition to the two we already have examined. According to Scripture, hell will destroy completely and forever. According to Tertullian, hell will torment forever. According to Origen, hell will purify and restore.

Chrysostom (349-407) means "Golden-Mouth" in Greek and he was eloquent even when woefully wrong. For example, he preached that Jesus sent the apostles into the world "to bring to us *the glad tidings of the soul's immortality,* and the eternal life of the body." He preached about people in hell "ever burning but not burnt up."

St. Augustine

Augustine (354-430), often called "St. Augustine," was a worldly and immoral man well into his adult years. A divine intervention was important in his conversion. Afterward, he became a chief theologian for defining and interpreting Christian doctrine. He devoted Book 21 of his massive *City of God* to a discussion of hell, coming down in support of Tertullian's theory and rejecting Origen's view. Augustine's endorsement of everlasting torment practically guaranteed that Tertullian's interpretation would become Catholic orthodoxy, and it did.

Anselm

We move next to Anselm of Canterbury (died 1117). His contribution to the doctrine of hell included a calculus of finitude and infinity. Because God is an infinite being and humans are finite, a sin against God by a human deserves infinite punishment. But, Anselm said, the only way a finite human can suffer infinite punishment is to suffer torment forever. Anselm's whole argument on this subject reflects the feudal law of his time, which measured degree of guilt and punishment by the relative standing of victim and perpetrator.

The whole theory was based on respect of persons, something forbidden by God in both Old and New Testaments. But even if Anselm's argument rested on solid principles, his conclusion would not necessarily follow, as a seventeenth century Reformed theologian named Herman Witsius later pointed out. If a finite human died in his or her entirety, so that nothing remained alive, and if that entire person died forever, Witsius said that would be infinite (which means "unlimited") punishment—just as surely as everlasting torment would be infinite punishment. Therefore, Anselm's argument does not require endless torment.[22]

Aquinas

St. Thomas Aquinas (died 1274) reconstructed Catholic doctrine on an Aristotelian philosophical base. Because the body follows the impulses of the soul, it bears less guilt for sin. Therefore it is proper for the soul to enter hell upon death and begin to suffer, while the body waits for the resurrection to join the soul in hell. This line of thought ignores the biblical picture of a general resurrection of all the dead, who do not go to reward or punishment until the resurrection and judgment have happened.

Reformation[23]

In the Reformation period, Martin Luther expressed himself often in terms of soul-sleeping and no conscious intermediate state, as well as questioning or denying the arguments for the immortality of the soul. Catholic Sir Thomas More took issue with Luther and William Tyndale came to his defense. Meanwhile, the Anabaptists were teaching no conscious intermediate state, natural human mortality, and the destruction of the wicked in hell.

Calvin wrote his first religious book against the Anabaptists on these issues. Titled *Psychopannychia*, which means "the soul never sleeps but is awake the whole night long," the volume accused the Anabaptists of getting their doctrines from hell, stated that their name alone is enough to damn anything they say, and many other intemperate and inflammatory statements.

When Luther recognized Calvin's vehemence on these points, he became quiet, leaving the Anabaptists standing alone in the world, and everyone else—Catholic, Reformed, and perhaps also Lutheran—hating and persecuting the Anabaptists.

Heinrich Bullinger wrote Calvin's ideas on these topics (which were Catholic orthodoxy) into the Second Helvetic Confession of 1566. That became a model for the Westminster theologians later in England.

The fundamentalist/modernist controversy occupied attention in America the first half of the twentieth century. The modernists denied heaven and hell altogether. The fundamentalists insisted that heaven and hell both are real. But the fundamentalists also insisted that hell will be exactly like the traditional hell of unending conscious torment. And they were so sure of themselves on this point that they looked with total suspicion on anyone who even raised a question about unending conscious torment, or who suggested that the Bible might actually teach something else.

The doctrine of everlasting torment was the direct descendant of the doctrine of immortal souls. Once the idea of everlasting torment was accepted and established, the church explained every Scripture to match the accepted doctrine, even when that meant creating an explanation that seemed to say the opposite of what the Scripture itself seemed to say. Many denominations, schools, and other institutions wrote unending torment into their doctrinal statements and confessions of faith.

> ## Everlasting torment: Pillar 4
>
> ### IMMORTALITY OF THE SOUL
>
> Pillar Four of the traditionalist doctrine states that the immortality of the soul requires unending conscious torment unless those in hell are restored to God and join him in heaven.

47   CONNECTING THE DOTS

As late as 1886, W. G. T. Shedd expressed the common opinion, held almost unanimously for as many as eighteen centuries, when he wrote:

> But irrepressible and universal as it is, the doctrine of man's immortality is an astonishing one, and difficult to entertain. For it means that every frail finite man is to be as long-enduring as the infinite and eternal God; that there will no more be an end to the existence of the man who died today than there will be of the Deity who made him. God is denominated "The Ancient of Days." But every immortal spirit that ever dwelt in a human body will also be an "ancient of days" . . . . Yes, man must exist. He has no option. Necessity is laid upon him. He cannot extinguish himself. He cannot cease to be.[24]

Today, teachers of Bible and theology in almost any accredited college or seminary know that the idea of immortal souls imprisoned in mortal bodies does not come from the Bible. Yet many fine people—professors, preachers, and pastors included—have not realized the pivotal role of that truth in the present rethinking of hell.

These men and women have been taught that hell will involve ever-lasting torment. Many of them do not know that the idea of everlasting torment was inferred from the false assumption that every human being has an immortal soul. Because they are unaware of that connection, they have not yet seen reason to abandon everlasting torment—even though they no longer believe in the immortality of the soul.

When they do make that connection, they are freed to speak of final options as the Bible does, in terms of *life* and *death*. When they do, they can let "death" mean *death* and not *eternal life in misery.*

Most of the historical details in this chapter were new to me as I "discovered" them during the year of research. However, it came as no surprise to me that the Bible does not teach the immortality of the soul, but teaches instead that human immortality is God's gift to the saved, given in the resurrection to them alone.

As it happened, while in graduate school I had read several "block-buster" books that opened gates to new paths of theological understanding based on the Word of God. One of the most profound and influential books was *Immortality of the Soul or Resurrection of the Dead? The Witness of the New Testament,* by Oscar Cullmann, published in 1958. In a mere sixty undersized pages, Cullmann convincingly shows that the concept of immortal souls is unbiblical and that it sprang from Greek philosophy and not from divine revelation.

Although that truth had hit me like a tornado when I read Cullmann a full decade earlier, when I was beginning the research project for Robert Brinsmead in the late 1970s, I still did not fully grasp its implication for the doctrine of hell. That revelation waited for documentary evidence from Tertullian himself, proving that he based his new doctrine of unending conscious torment directly on his older belief that every person has an immortal soul.

That discovery, more than any other single surprise I encountered, became the *Eureka!* moment in my research project on final punishment. Actor Mackenzie Astin captures and recreates the sheer excitement of that moment in the 2012 feature film "Hell and Mr. Fudge."

48 PROVIDENTIAL— Press and more

Earlier I described some of the anxieties that attacked me when I began to consider writing a book to share the amazing things the research project was uncovering. I had used the proper scholarly tools in doing the research and had used them properly. But peace was not quick in coming. I felt as though I was wrestling with an invisible opponent. The dialogue was fierce and unremitting.

> ME: *I must share this with my brothers and sisters.*
>
> VOICE: But the church has always said otherwise!
>
> ME: *I have prayed for guidance.*
>
> VOICE: This is what Seventh-day Adventists teach.
>
> ME: *Might it be that God has been preparing me for this very task and time?*
>
> VOICE: Why should he use *you?*
>
> ME: *I have done the work properly. Now I need to trust the results.*
>
> VOICE: The whole evangelical world will turn against you.
>
> ME: *I risk God's displeasure if I remain silent.*

In retrospect, now more than thirty years later, it appears that God's hand has been on this project from the very beginning until this day. *The Fire*

That Consumes was released in 1982 by Verdict Publications, Brinsmead's publishing name. The first printing sold out in five months and Brinsmead wrote to say that he was giving me all publishing rights to my book. That was exceedingly generous on his part, because he had invested years of work and many thousands of dollars on the research and actual publication. His only request was that if I reprinted it, I would maintain the high quality of workmanship evident in his first printing. Of course, I was eager to do that very thing already. All I needed in order to go forward was $10,000.00. It had as well been a million, so far as I was concerned.

My family had recently moved to Houston, Texas, where I had been hired as founding editor of an interdenominational Christian newspaper called *The Good Newspaper.* We had also joined the Bering Drive Church of Christ, Now I sought counsel from the church elders—"asking for ideas, not money," I truthfully told them. If God had plans for this book, he would make a way.

After hearing me out, two of the elders commented that they were unfamiliar with the message of my book but they believed in Christian scholarship. On that basis, they offered to co-sign a note for me to borrow an amount that would cover the costs of a second printing. I thanked God, and also his two special agents whom, now thirty years later, I still consider my partners in this project.

After some thought, I decided to publish *The Fire That Consumes* under a publishing name of its own. Now I needed just the right name. One Sunday morning not long after, I was guest preacher at a church in southwest Houston, and my wife and I were talking about possible trade names as we drove to the church. Just then we passed a billboard sign advertising Providence Homes Builders. Almost immediately, we said together: "Providential Press." I filed the name in the Assumed Names offices of the state of Texas and of Harris County, and Providential Press became a reality. No entity ever had a name more appropriate!

Soon after, the Evangelical Book Club chose *The Fire That Consumes* as an Alternate Selection, which gave it tremendous exposure. The fact that it had a foreword by F. F. Bruce, one of the most highly-respected Bible scholars of the twentieth century, lent enormous credence to this unknown book and to its unknown author.

Canadian Baptist theologian Clark Pinnock, a dear brother who possessed a childlike trust in God and a keen intellectual creativity on a host of issues, wrote me to say how happy he was to have a non-Adventist book to recommend on this topic. And, from a somewhat different perspective, the Adventist folk were equally happy—and for the same reason.

Dr. Desmond Ford, another Australian theologian with two PhDs, one under F. F. Bruce, contacted me and offered to help make the book known. Ford was a Seventh-day Adventist whose ministerial credentials had been pulled because he challenged a unique doctrine of the denomination on biblical grounds. Unlike Brinsmead, Ford chose to remain in the denomination, where he continues to teach and preach as invited.

I wrote a four-page brochure about *The Fire That Consumes*, titled "A Loving Challenge to the Evangelical Church," and Ford's ministry "Good News Unlimited" printed and mailed it to three thousand members of the Evangelical Theological Society. Approximately three hundred members ordered the book from that mailing—a phenomenal response by direct mail advertising standards.

49   DOORS OPEN FOR THE WORD

Every year since its publication, *The Fire That Consumes* has been used by God to open doors for the message of life only in Christ. That is really the positive biblical message to which the final destruction of the wicked is the shadow side.

Acts of the Apostles reports how the apostles went everywhere telling the good news of Jesus Christ, whom God raised from the dead and in whom we may enjoy eternal life. Conditional immortality is about life. Death is the consequence of rejecting life.

With the publication of *The Fire That Consumes* came invitations to lecture at churches of all sorts, pastors' conferences, retreats, regional and national conferences, seminaries, and schools. These included both Fuller Theological Seminary in California and Gordon-Conwell Theological Seminary in Massachusetts, two of the top evangelical seminaries anywhere, both of which I highly respected and was honored to be associated with.

Invitations came from Saskatchewan and Ontario provinces in Canada; from Portland, Oregon to San Diego on the West Coast; from St. Simon Island, Georgia and Nashville, Tennessee and states between. One weekend I spoke in Massachusetts on Friday night, in Central New Hampshire on Saturday, in Southern New Hampshire on Sunday morning, and Northern New Hampshire on Sunday night.

In August of 2000, my wife and I were invited to spend ten days in New Zealand, where our hosts had arranged for me to lecture, preach, and teach in two seminaries, a major state university, three churches representative of two denominations, and a Christian bookstore. The trip was rewarding for the joy of ministry, considerable sightseeing, making new friends, and—not insignificant—leaving Houston, Texas in August for a country where Christmas comes in the middle of summer and August can see snowfall.

Typically, reactions include a spectrum of agreement, neutrality, and disapproval. Several people almost always tell me they have been studying this subject for themselves and have concluded, as I did, that the wicked will be totally burned up. These folks appreciate the affirmation. Closely akin to these are the listeners to whom these ideas are new but instantly attractive. A well-known woman who hosts a major evangelical radio and television program looked me in the eye and said, "This certainly sounds more like God, doesn't it."

The largest category, in terms of reaction, is the group of people who express gratitude and interest regarding the stimulation, and who pledge to continue their study. And it is not uncommon for at least one person to exit a meeting with a hostile glare and a verbal reproof.

I cannot say how many people have told me, in person or by mail or email, how much this message blessed them personally after years of anxiety created by the traditional doctrine of unending torment. Usually their concern was for loved ones thought to be unsaved. These believers did not try to avoid hell's reality. They simply sought an understanding that sounded more just and fair than the majority tradition provided. Many of these brothers and sisters told me that *The Fire That Consumes* had saved their sanity, their faith—or, in some cases, their lives.

Others have related that the good news of life in Christ has revitalized their ministry. I had never known the extent to which the traditional doctrine of everlasting torment hinders the gospel, robs seekers of faith, and closes hearts to the real "good news" that Jesus gives life and has defeated death for those who belong to him.

As a basis for changing our minds, discussions about what helps or hinders evangelism do not belong at the front end of a book or a conference, but at the close. The first question is *"What does the Bible say?"* Only then can we legitimately talk about the desirable or undesirable effects of a doctrine on our work or that of other people. All comments in this book concerning the supposed practical effects of any viewpoint on the subject of final punishment should be read with that caveat in mind.

50 AN EVANGELICAL CLIMATE CHANGE

After being labeled "cultic" and "heretical" by traditionalists for hundreds of years, believers who question unending conscious torment are enjoying the prospect of an evangelical climate change attributable only to a work of grace. Winds of change were first spotted in 1975, the year that InterVarsity Press published *The Goodness of God* by John W. Wenham, a scholar-priest in Oxford. The book contained a chapter on hell as a moral difficulty in Christianity as viewed by many. The problem is not hell as such—retributive suffering is arguably not only moral but absolutely necessary for the maintenance of a peaceful and just society.

The problem is the traditional hell of everlasting conscious torment, an idea many find inconsistent with both the love and justice of God. Wenham counseled restraint in abandoning the traditional doctrine of hell, but he urged that every reader carefully consider the biblical evidence for conditional immortality. This was apparently the first book critical of the traditionalist hell from a mainstream American evangelical publisher.

With the publication of *Two Views of Hell* (Fudge and Peterson, 2000), InterVarsity Press further acknowledged, by its even-handed language, that the question whether hell involves everlasting torment or total destruction is open to discussion and disagreement among evangelical Christians. The publisher's description on the back cover identified the authors as "two evangelical theologians," stating that "some evangelicals" hold to everlasting torment, while "others" believe in total destruction. In the past, the traditionalist view would have been described as "the orthodox view" or some equivalent.

The conference of 450 evangelical theologians in 1989 at Trinity Evangelical Divinity School near Chicago, mentioned earlier, illustrates both sides of the broadening issue presently being hashed out. On the one hand, we can say that as *recently* as 1989, a group of theologians attempted to eliminate from the evangelical tent by definition all who reject the traditionalist view of conscious unending torment. On the other hand, we can say that as *early* as 1989, such an attempt was unsuccessful, if barely so.

In the providence of God, *The Fire That Consumes* has earned a place of respect and attention since 1982, and authors frequently interact with it at the highest scholarly levels. It is quoted, discussed, agreed with, and disagreed with in *The New International Greek New Testament Commentary* series and in *The New International Commentary on the New Testament* series, as well as *The New Oxford Handbook on Eschatology.*

As I write this book, *The Fire That Consumes* is on a senior theology reading list at The University of Saint Andrews, Scotland. At least two doctoral dissertations have been written on some aspect of the book, one at Oxford University.

Christianity Today calls *The Fire That Consumes* "the standard reference on annihilationism." In his foreword to the third edition of *The Fire That Consumes,* Richard Bauckham of Cambridge University predicts it "likely to remain a standard work to which everyone engaged with this issue will constantly return."

On a popular level, the story of Edward and Sara Faye (Locke), particularly in relation to the research project that led to writing *The Fire That*

Consumes, has inspired a full-length feature dramatic movie set for release in 2012. Titled "Hell and Mr. Fudge," the film features Mackenzie Astin as the adult Edward and Keri Lynn Pratt as Sara Faye. For more information and to see a trailer, go to www.hellandmrfudge.com .

Gone are the days when no respectable evangelical scholar admitted to questioning the biblical basis of everlasting conscious torment. The three men who have contributed forewords to editions of *The Fire That Consumes* bring enough *gravitas* and moral authority to the table to legitimize the question, even if they were alone in the matter.

But they are far from alone. The same generation that produced such illustrious scholars as F. F. Bruce and John W. Wenham, also included Dale Moody, E. Earle Ellis, Homer Hailey, Philip E. Hughes, John Stott, Stephen Travis, Michael Green, and I. Howard Marshall. To a man, these all publicly rejected the traditional hell and its unending conscious torment. The only man of international reputation from that generation who is widely known for his defense of the traditional view is J. I. Packer.

Dr. Packer is now retired from Regent College in Vancouver, where his successor is John Stackhouse, Jr., a recently declared conditionalist. Respected evangelical scholars from my own generation—that falls between Packer's and Stackhouse's—also rejected the traditional hell because they did not find it in the Bible. Among these are Clark Pinnock, John McRay, Claude Mariottini, Christopher Marshall, Tom Robinson, Richard Bauckham, and N.T. Wright.

Already a younger generation of devout scholars are publishing their biblical reasons for rejecting the traditional view of eternal torment. In addition to John Stackhouse, Jr., this group includes J. Gregory Crofford, John R. Franke, and Gregory Boyd,

When wrestling with the "Voice" back in the late 1970s, I regarded it a fact beyond dispute that no one would read a five-hundred-page scholarly book on the subject of final punishment. No one had heard of me, so authorship was no appeal. I remembered those thoughts earlier this year when a national Christian newspaper ran two stories about me and my book. One story title identified me as "one of the world's foremost scholars on hell," while a second headline promoted me to "Top Scholar on Hell."

Those kinds of voices can be fully as misleading and harmful as the first kind, I reflected. Better not to pay attention to either.

The bottom line, which I remind myself every day, is that this whole enterprise is not about me anyway. It is about God and his character and glory and praise. When we remember that, and act accordingly, there are no limits on what he can accomplish.

When I climbed the steps to the elevated pulpit in September 2011 to present a lecture sponsored by the Lanier Theological Library in Houston, Texas, my first sentence was a question: "Who would ever have thought that eight-hundred people would come out on a Saturday night to hear an hour-long lecture on hell?" The second sentence said it all. "But by the grace of God, here we are, so let us proceed!"

Indeed . . . "by the grace of God." And whether he has us ministering to eight people or 80,000 people, let us always remember that everything is grace. And then, in that grace, let us proceed.

51 BY THE GREATER WEIGHT

For the moment, I remove the mantle of theology and assume the cloak of a lawyer, my other chosen profession. In that role, I offer these closing thoughts.

You have now heard the cases for conditional immortality and for everlasting conscious torment. If you have ever served on a jury, you are acquainted with the concept of a standard of proof.

You will recall that the standard of proof refers to that standard of evidence necessary for the jury to render a lawful verdict, and also the sufficient basis for an appellate court to sustain the verdict against legal challenge. No doubt you also remember that the standard of proof in civil court differs from the standard in criminal court in at least two important respects.

First, a criminal conviction requires the jurors to reach a unanimous decision, and to reach such decision "beyond a reasonable doubt." In other words, every juror must be convinced not only that the evidence supports the Defendant's guilt rather than innocence but, much more, each juror must believe that the evidence supports it so strongly that it cannot reasonably be interpreted any other way.

The standard of proof in a civil case is quite different. A verdict can be rendered without unanimous vote. More important, in a civil case, the judge instructs the jury to render a verdict based on "the greater weight and preponderance of the evidence." This means that the scales of justice need to be tilted only the slightest in favor of one party or the other.

Which of these jury standards do you normally use when deciding a disputed teaching? Do you insist that every relevant verse in the Bible on the subject must favor a particular point of view for you to accept that viewpoint as valid? Criminal-trial logic is not suitable for most doctrinal disputes or interpretations of Scripture. Few teachings in the Bible are that clear-cut or black-and-white. Usually there is some ambiguity. If we think about it for a moment, we realize that is why there is a dispute in the first place.

Now that you have read this book, it is time to ask which view of hell is supported by the greater weight and preponderance of the evidence. Taking all the biblical evidence into account, do you consider one explanation of hell to be more likely than the others? Which explanation makes the most sense? Does one seem more like God? Is it the view of hell as a place of unending conscious torment? Is it hell as a fire that purifies and reforms? Is it the understanding of hell as the fire that consumes?

God has revealed what we need to know. Not necessarily enough to satisfy our curiosity or to answer all our questions. He reveals all we need to know to please him each new "today." As we live by his light, our lives progressively conform to his character. We are God's born-again children, destined to live with the Father now in unity, service, and praise. And, when mortality is replaced with immortality and all that is broken in this universe is redeemed as part of new heavens and earth, we will enjoy him forever, together, without end.

FOR FURTHER STUDY

For a thorough investigation of everything the Bible says about the destiny of the lost, you might wish to read *The Fire That Consumes*, the book that resulted from Edward's research project at the center of the story in this book. Exhaustive in scope and scholarly in approach, this book has helped to stir a worldwide rethinking of the doctrine of hell among evangelical Christians and is now widely considered to be a classic in the field.

An Alternate Selection of the Evangelical Book Club in the first edition (reprint of original available from iUniverse.com), this landmark book is now brought up to date in a thoroughly revised third edition from wipfandstock.com or wherever books are sold. If you order from anyone other than wipfandstock.com be sure you specify the third edition, published by Cascade Books/Wipf and Stock, with foreword by Richard Bauckham.

If you want to consider both sides as presented by proponents of each, you will enjoy *Two Views of Hell: A Biblical and Theological Dialogue*, by Edward William Fudge (conditionalist view) and Robert A. Peterson (traditionalist view) from InterVarsity Press (2000). Each man presents the case for his own position, and each man responds to the other. Available at your favorite booksellers.

In September 2011, Edward presented a 69-minute lecture on the subject of final punishment, sponsored by the Lanier Theological Library in Houston, Texas. In the lecture, he summarize the material discussed in depth in *The Fire That Consumes*. The lecture was professionally recorded, and the sponsoring library has made it available for viewing online at no charge, or for purchase on a DVD. Just go to www. LanierTheologicalLibrary.org and click under "Videos." Welcome to the conversation!

A MOST SURPRISING QUIZ ON HELL

The Bible warns about the judgment of God and banishment to hell. But did you know that many popular ideas about hell actually sprang from ancient pagan myths and not from the Word of God?

In the following quiz, see if you can spot the biblical truth and the traditions of men. After the quiz, you'll find the correct answers—and references to appropriate biblical passages for further study.

---

1. **According to the Bible, the human being is:**
   a) a mortal body housing an immortal soul;
   b) a tale told by an idiot, full of sound and fury;
   c) a perishable creature wholly dependent on God for existence.

---

2. **Two historical events which biblical writers use most often to illustrate God's final judgment against the wicked are:**
   a) expulsion from Eden and the collapse of the Tower of Babel;
   b) the fall of Jerusalem and the defeat of the Spanish Armada;
   c) the Flood and the destruction of Sodom and Gomorrah.

---

3. **Based on an actual event, the Bible uses the expression "eternal fire" to signify:**
   a) fire that destroys forever (Sodom and Gomorrah);
   b) fire that cannot destroy what is put in it (Shadrach, Meshach & Abednego);
   c) fire that continues to burn indefinitely (the Burning Bush of Moses).

4. The "brimstone" in "fire and brimstone" is:
a) a symbol of terrible torture;
b) burning sulfur that suffocates and destroys;
c) a preserving agent that keeps someone alive forever.

5. Throughout the Bible, "gnashing of teeth" denotes:
a) excruciating pain and agony;
b) gingivitis;
c) extreme anger and hostility.

6. When the Bible portrays "smoke rising" to warn of judgment, we should think of:
a) people suffering horrible pain;
b) a completed desolation or annihilation;
c) a closed arena when cigarettes were still allowed.

7. When Scripture speaks of smoke rising "forever," it signifies:
a) a destruction that will be irreversible;
b) conscious torment that never ends;
c) a battery-powered rabbit that short circuited.

8. The "worm" in the expression "worm that dies not" is:
a) a maggot that feeds on something dead;
b) a symbol for a pained conscience;
c) a figure of speech standing for everlasting agony in torment.

9. Throughout the Bible, the expression "unquenchable fire" always signifies:
a) fire which burns forever but never burns up what is put in it;
b) fire which comes from a volcano;
c) fire which is irresistible and therefore consumes entirely.

10. The Old Testament's final description of the end of sinners states that:
a) God will put fire and worms in their flesh and they will feel their pain forever;
b) they will be ashes under the soles of the feet of the righteous;
c) neither of the above.

11. **John the Baptist warned of "unquenchable fire," by which Jesus would:**
    a) burn up the "chaff";
    b) torment the lost forever and never let them die;
    c) purge sinners of all evil and then send them to heaven.

12. **Jesus compared the end of the wicked to:**
    a) someone burning chaff, dead trees or weeds;
    b) a house destroyed by a hurricane or someone crushed under a boulder;
    c) all the above.

13. **Jesus personally described gehenna (hell) as a place where:**
    a) God is able to destroy both soul and body;
    b) God will perpetuate the soul in everlasting agony;
    c) Satan reigns over his evil subjects and tortures damned humans.

14. **The phrase "eternal punishment" signifies:**
    a) punishment which occurs in the Age to Come rather than during this life;
    b) eternal life in horrible agony and pain;
    c) punishment which has everlasting results;
    d) (a) and (c) but not (b).

15. **The context and "punch line" of the story of the Rich Man and Lazarus talk about:**
    a) what happens to the wicked after resurrection and judgment;
    b) the urgency of responding to God while there is opportunity;
    c) details about the "intermediate state" between death and resurrection.

16. **Throughout his writings, Paul says that the lost will:**
    a) go to hell and burn alive forever;
    b) die, perish, and be punished with eternal destruction;
    c) go to heaven but hate every minute of it.

17. **The New Testament uses the adjective "immortal" to describe:**
    a) the soul of every person, good or evil;

b) the resurrection bodies of the saved but not of the lost;

c) no human being now or hereafter.

18. The Jewish-Christian books of Hebrews and James contrast salvation with:

a) unending conscious pain;

b) inescapable destruction;

c) going "gently into that good night."

19. Peter's epistles say that the lost will:

a) be burned to ashes like Sodom and Gomorrah;

b) perish like brute beasts;

c) both the above.

20. John interprets his vision in Revelation of a "lake of fire" as:

a) a picture of indescribable, everlasting torture;

b) a place Eskimos might like to visit;

c) the second death.

CHECK YOUR ANSWERS BY THE BIBLE

1. I hope you marked (c). According to the Bible, the human being is a perishable creature wholly dependent on God for existence.

The notion that your mortal body houses some kind of immortal soul sprang from the pagan Greeks and was popularized by the philosophers Socrates and Plato. The "tale told by an idiot, full of sound and fury" line originated with Shakespeare's fictional Macbeth, not with the Word of God.

Genesis 2:7; Psalms 103:14-16; Romans 6:23; 1 Tim. 6:16.

2. Again the correct answer is (c). Biblical writers point back to the Flood and to the destruction of Sodom and Gomorrah to illustrate the fate awaiting the lost.

Adam and Eve walked away alive after their expulsion from Eden, something no one cast into hell will ever do, and the Bible does not say the Tower of Babel collapsed. Jerusalem's fall and the defeat of Spain's navy armada don't qualify here, either.

On the Flood, see Genesis 6-9 and 2 Peter 3:5-7. Concerning Sodom and Gomorrah, see Genesis 19:24-29 and 2 Peter 2:6 and Jude 7.

3. In the Bible, the expression "eternal fire" signifies choice (a), fire that destroys forever, as with Sodom and Gomorrah.

Popular tradition says hell will be like Moses' Burning Bush which never went out, or like the non-consuming furnace into which their enemies threw Shadrach, Meshach and Abednego. However, the Bible warns that hell is a consuming fire which destroys both body and soul.

Jude 7; Matthew 25:41; Matthew 10:28.

4. This time (b) is biblical. The "brimstone" in the expression "fire and brimstone" is burning sulfur that suffocates and destroys.

The figure comes from the destruction of Sodom, which was incinerated without a trace. God is love, not an eternal torturer. The Bible really means it when it says the wages of sin is death!

Genesis 19:24-25, 29; Deuteronomy 29:22-23; Psalms 11:6; Ezekiel 38:22; Revelation 14:10;Romans 6:23.

5. Surprise! Throughout the Bible, "gnashing of teeth" denotes (c) extreme anger and hostility.

The picture of people grinding their teeth in unending torment owes more to Dante's Inferno than it does to the Bible. We learn about gingivitis, of course, from a television commercial for a brand of mouthwash.

Job 16:9; Psalms 35:16; Psalms 37:12; Psalms 112:10; Lamentations 2:16; Acts 7:54; Matthew 13:43, 49-50; Matthew 22:13-14; Matthew 24:50-51; Matthew 25:30; Luke 13:28.

6. Again (b) is biblical. Smoke rising symbolizes a completed desolation or annihilation, if we let Scripture interpret itself.

This figure of speech also originates with the annihilation of Sodom and Gomorrah, and appears in both the Old and New Testaments afterward. Hell might well involve conscious pain, but conscious suffering will be according to God's perfect justice and will stop with the death of both body and soul in hell. (You didn't guess the one about cigarettes anyway, did you.)

Genesis 19:27-28; Isaiah 34:10-15; Revelation 14:11; Revelation 18:17-18; Malachi 4:1-3.

7. See for yourself! When Scripture speaks of smoke rising "forever," it signifies (a) destruction that will be irreversible.

That battery-powered rabbit came from the television commercials—it is no more biblical than the other choice, the notion of unending conscious torment.

Isaiah 34:10-15; Revelation 14:11.

8. Another big surprise for most folks! The "worm" in the expression "worm that dies not" is (a) a maggot that feeds on something dead until there is nothing left on which to feed.

The idea of everlasting agony in torment originated with former pagan Greek philosophers who also thought human beings had a "soul" which will never die. More tender-hearted traditionalists later defined the "worm" as a pained conscience. If they had read Isaiah 66:24 in context, they could have avoided the confusion to start with.

Isaiah 66:24; Mark 9:47-48.

9. This time (c) is correct. The expression "unquenchable fire" in the Bible always signifies fire which cannot be resisted and which therefore consumes entirely.

Long after Christ, certain church fathers invented the doctrine of hell as a fire which burns forever but never burns up what is put in it.

Isaiah 1:31; Jeremiah 4:4; Jeremiah 17:27; Ezekiel 20:47-48; Amos 5:5-6; Matthew 3:12. Contrast human fire which can be quenched or put out, mentioned in Hebrews 11:34.

10. No surprise here if you chose (b). The Old Testament's final book describes the end of sinners as ashes under the soles of the feet of the righteous.

Long after Malachi, the apocryphal book of Judith introduced the non-scriptural idea that God will put fire and worms in people's flesh so they will feel pain forever.

Malachi 4:1-3.

11. John the Baptist warned of "unquenchable fire," by which Jesus would (a) burn up the "chaff". Not surprising, since fire that cannot be extinguished (quenched) does exactly what we expect fire to do!

Missing this biblical truth, some later theologians claimed that God will torment the lost forever and never let them die, while others theorized that God will purge sinners of all evil and then send them to heaven. Both theories have modern advocates, but neither of them reflects the Bible's teaching.

Matthew 3:12.

12. Jesus compared the end of the wicked to someone burning chaff, dead trees or weeds, and also said it will be like a house destroyed by a hurricane or someone crushed under falling rock. Check (c) here to be correct.

Matthew 3:12; Matthew 7:19; Matthew 13:30, 40; Matthew 7:27; Luke 20:17-18.

13. Choice (a) is accurate on this one. Jesus personally described gehenna (hell) as a place where God can destroy both soul and body—the entire person.

The just and loving God of the Bible who loved sinners all the way to the Cross will certainly not perpetuate the soul in everlasting agony. On the other hand, if you pictured Satan reigning over his evil subjects and torturing damned humans, you might be watching too much late-night television!

Matthew 10:28.

14. If you selected choice (d), you are right on target. By describing hell's punishment as "eternal," the Bible tells us that it is a punishment which occurs in the Age to Come rather than during this life, and also that its results will be everlasting.

You'll find nothing in Scripture about eternal life in horrible agony and pain. Jesus warns of everlasting punishment--which Paul further explains as everlasting destruction.

Matthew 25:46; 2 Thessalonians 1:9.

15. The context and "punch line" of the story of the Rich Man and Lazarus concern (b) the urgency of responding to God while there is opportunity

When they read this passage carefully, most people are surprised to find that the context of Jesus' parable has nothing to do with what happens to the wicked after resurrection and judgment, or even about a so-called "intermediate state" (which is not necessarily the same as what happens after resurrection and final judgment).

See Luke 16:9-16 for the context, and Luke 16:31 for the "punch line."

16. It's choice (b) again. Throughout his writings, Paul says that the lost will: (b) die, perish, and be punished with eternal destruction.

If you picked choice (a) "go to hell and burn alive forever," you will really be surprised when you look for anything like that in Paul's writings. Choice (c) is wrong, since all who finally inhabit God's eternal kingdom will enjoy every "minute" of unending eternity!

Romans 6:23; Romans 2:12; 1 Thessalonians 5:2-3; 2 Thessalonians 1:9; 1 Corinthians 3:17; Philippians 1:28; Philippians 3:19.

17. The New Testament uses the adjective "immortal" to describe (b) the resurrection bodies of the saved but not of the lost.

Some philosophers in Paul's day taught that every person has an immortal soul—a doctrine which later crept into the Christian church but is now increasingly rejected as unbiblical. Still others said no one will ever be "immortal" or deathless. Scripture rejects both those errors, when it declares that there is life only in Christ but promises that all who truly trust him will live forever! You will always be correct to remember that the Bible always ascribes immortality to the saved, never to the lost; always in the resurrection, never now; and always in a glorified body, never as a disembodied "soul" or "spirit."

1 Corinthians 15:54-57; 2 Timothy 1:10; 1 John 5:11-13.

18. Did you choose (b)? Good for you! The Jewish-Christian books of Hebrews and James do indeed contrast salvation with inescapable destruction.

Read every word and you'll never find a hint of unending conscious pain. Going "gently into that good night" is poetic but comes from Welsh poet Dylan Thomas rather than the Bible.

Hebrews 10:27, 39; Hebrews 12:25, 29; James 4:12; James 5:3, 5, 20.

19. Choice (c) is correct. Peter's epistles clearly say that the lost will be burned to ashes like Sodom and Gomorrah and will perish like brute beasts.

2 Peter 2:6, 12; 2 Peter 3:6-9.

20. John is careful to define the "lake of fire" in Revelation as (c) the second death.

Read from Genesis to Revelation and you'll never find a picture of indescribable, everlasting torture. Does that come as a surprise?

Revelation 20:14; Revelation 21:8.

ENDNOTES

1. John Gerstner, *Repent or Perish* (Ligonier, Pa.: Soli Deo Gloria, 1990), 64.

2. Mark Twain, *The Adventures of Huckleberry Finn*, 3-4. Online: http://etext.virginia.edu/etcbin/toccer-new2?id=Twa2Huc.sgm&images=images/modeng&data=/texts/english/modeng/parsed&tag=public&part=1&division=div1

3. "Heaven and Hell" (September 4, 1855), *The New Park Street Pulpit*. Online: http://www.spurgeon.org/sermons/0039.htm.

4. A. W. Pink, *Eternal Punishment* (Swengel, Pa.: Reiner, n.d.), 29-30.

5. Gerstner, *Repent or Perish*, 31-32.

6. Ibid., 32. Original underlined.

7. Traditionalist authors like to imagine that people who say that unending conscious torment is not found in the Bible are really motivated by the spirit of our age—a spirit of softness, fuzzy thinking, subjectivism, and the desire for a "kinder and gentler" doctrine that will be more inviting to sinners who need to hear hard preaching instead.

The truth is exactly the opposite. Those most engaged in "watering down" hell's torments, those most eagerly explaining away its terrors, are not conditionalists who reject unending conscious torment. The folks who seem most eager to find a kinder and gentler doctrine are the traditionalists themselves, embarrassed beyond words by the terror-inspiring, "hell-fire-and-damnation" preaching of past centuries by men like Wesley and Spurgeon and Pink. These good brothers and sisters need to realize that their problem is not a *harsh delivery* but a *mistaken message*. The only effective solution to their problem will not be a kinder and gentler tone, or even a watered-down message, but the total rejection of the idea (found nowhere in Scripture) that God will keep the unredeemed alive forever for punishment of any kind.

8. "Davy" is a fictional name for a composite character.

9. Of course, only God knows the answer to that question with certainty. I do not ask the question for information, but for stimulation.

10. Bertrand Russell, "Why I Am Not A Christian," a lecture delivered on March 6, 1927 to the National Secular Society, South London Branch, at Battersea Town Hall, U.K. Published in pamphlet form in that same year, later the title chapter in *Why I*

Am Not a Christian and Other Essays, edited by Paul Edwards (New York: Simon & Schuster,1957). Online: http://users.drew.edu/~jlenz/whynot.html .

11. Antony Flew and Thomas Warren, *The Warren-Flew Debate on the Existence of God* (Jonesboro, Ark.: National Christian Press, 1977), 84-86.

12. Charles Hodge (1797-1878), in a letter to a "Dr. Cunningham" dated August 24, 1857, quoted in Archibald Alexander Hodge, *The Life of Charles Hodge* (New York: Scribner's, 1880), 430. Online: http://www.archive.org/stream/ lifecharleshodg00hodggoog#page/n452/mode/2up/.

13. If you want all the scholarly details about the Greek and Hebrew words translated "eternal," see chapter four in Edward Fudge, *The Fire That Consumes: A Biblical and Historical Study of the Doctrine of Final Punishment*, 3ʳᵈ edition (Eugene, Ore.: Cascade Books/Wipf and Stock, 2011), 33-43.

14. For a footnoted summary of *sheol* in the Old Testament, see chapter five, titled "Sheol/Hades: Gravedom?" in *The Fire That Consumes,* 3ʳᵈ ed., 44-50.

15. Karel Hanhart, "The Intermediate State in the New Testament" (1996 doctoral dissertation, University of Amsterdam), 192-93.

16. Robert A. Morey, *Death and the Afterlife* (Minneapolis: Bethany, 1984), 30f, 84f,

17. Christopher W. Morgan, "Biblical Theology: Three Pictures of Hell," *Hell Under Fire*, ed. Christopher W. Morgan and Robert A. Peterson (Grand Rapids, Mich.: Zondervan, 2004), 140.

18. R. Albert Mohler, Jr., "Modern Theology: The Disappearance of Hell," *Hell Under Fire*, 17.

19. Strack and Billerbeck's original German quotation, its translation into English, and the original citation are all found in *The Fire That Consumes*, 3ʳᵈ ed., 115.

20. Hanns Lilje, *The Last Book of the Bible* (Philadelphia, Pa.: Muhlenberg Press, 1957), 146.

21. John Donne, "Death, Be Not Proud (Holy Sonnet 10)." Online: http://www. poets.org/viewmedia.php/prmMID/15836 .

22. See full quotation and discussion of Witsius' remarks in *The Fire That Consumes,* 3ʳᵈ ed., 306-07.

23. For direct quotations, specific details, and complete documentation on the Reformers and the doctrine of hell, see *The Fire That Consumes,* 3ʳᵈ ed., 309-28.

24. W. G. T. Shedd, *The Doctrine of Endless Punishment* (New York: Scribner's, 1886), 490.

EDWARD WILLIAM FUDGE is a Bible teacher, preacher, and licensed attorney living in Houston, Texas. His internet publication, gracEmail, regularly encourages thousands of believers around the world. He has ministered with churches of many denominations in the U.S., Canada, and New Zealand. He is the author of *Hebrews: Ancient Encouragement for Believers Today, The Fire That Consumes, The Divine Rescue, Two Views of Hell, The Sound of His Voice,* and other books. Edward and his wife Sara Faye have been married 45 years and have two children and five grandchildren.

MACKENZIE
ASTIN

KERI LYNN
PRATT

HELL and Mr. Fudge

A little story about a big lie.

For information contact LLT Productions
1-800-558-4478 or lltproductions@sbcglobal.net
Website: www.hellandmrfudge.com

CPSIA information can be obtained at www.ICGtesting.com
Printed in the USA
LVOW12n0903150315

430444LV00002B/2/P